THE BEADED OBJECT

*Making Gorgeous
Flowers & Other
Decorative Accents*

THE BEADED OBJECT

Making Gorgeous Flowers
& Other Decorative Accents

MARY JO HINEY

Sterling Publishing Co., Inc. New York
A Sterling / Chapelle Book

Library of Congress Cataloging-in-Publication Data Available

Chapelle:

Jo Packham, Owner

Cathy Sexton, Editor

Staff: Areta Bingham, Kass Burchett, Marilyn Goff, Holly Hollingsworth, Susan Jorgensen, Kimberly Maw, Barbara Milburn, Linda Orton, Karmen Quinney, Leslie Ridenour, Cindy Stoeckl, Gina Swapp, Sara Toliver

Photography: Kevin Dilley for Hazen Photography

To make the headbands shown on pages 2–3, use the basic instructions for the techniques on pages 21–22 (Lily of the Valley) and pages 74–75 (Garland).

We would like to thank the following companies for providing materials that were used in this publication: Art Accents, Artistic Wire, D & CC, Mill Hill, Ruban Et Fleur, and Scotticrafts.

If you have any questions or comments or would like information on specialty products featured in this book, please contact:
Chapelle, Ltd., Inc.,
P.O. Box 9252, Ogden, UT 84409
(801) 621-2777 • (801) 621-2788 Fax
e-mail: chapelle@chapelleltd.com
website: www.chapelleltd.com

*Mary Jo would like to extend
her heartfelt thanks
to Cathy Sexton
for the integrity
and artistry of her work
while editing this book,
adding to her bouquet of memories
many pleasant conversations.*

10 9 8 7 6 5 4 3 2

A Sterling/Chapelle Book

First paperback edition published in 2002 by
Sterling Publishing Company, Inc.
387 Park Avenue South, New York, N.Y. 10016
© 2001 by Mary Jo Hiney
Distributed in Canada by Sterling Publishing
℅ Canadian Manda Group, One Atlantic Avenue, Suite 105
Toronto, Ontario, Canada M6K 3E7
Distributed in Great Britain and Europe by Chrysalis Books
64 Brewery Road, London N7 9NT, England
Distributed in Australia by Capricorn Link (Australia) Pty. Ltd.
P.O. Box 704, Windsor, NSW 2756 Australia

Printed and Bound in China
All Rights Reserved

Sterling ISBN 0-8069-6090-6 Hardcover
0-8069-7435-4 Paperback

TABLE OF CONTENTS

Introduction

On your antiquing excursions, perhaps you've run across interesting arrangements of beadwork on wire, in the shape of flowers. It is an old tradition, created centuries ago by the peasants of France and northern Italy, and was most recently in vogue in the 1960s. When my piano teacher created a bouquet of beaded roses for my mom, it was I who was fascinated by them.

There are many wonderful forms to create with beaded wire and any flower imaginable can be made from the techniques showcased in these pages. But flowers are just the beginning. In addition to creating forms with beaded wire, think of the plain surfaces that are crying out for bead embellishment. This book is meant to provide a solid foundation for you from which you will grow in creating the beaded object.

Beads are magnificent diminutive objects, the array of which will leave you light-headed. Rather than being overwhelmed by the quantity of choices, focus on the small picture and expand your knowledge a little at a time.

Seed Beads

Seed beads range in size from a very petite 14/0 to a large 6/0. The standard seed bead size is 11/0. Color choices are extraordinary. Seed beads can be silver-lined, metallic, iris, transparent, transparent rainbow, frosted, opaque, color-lined, square-cut, and faceted. Seed beads can be purchased in strung hanks, or loose in containers of varying sizes. Almost all seed beads have holes, but there are tiny holeless seed beads available.

Petite Seed Beads

These 14/0 beads are very small and can be difficult to work with, but they add a wonderful, meticulous look to your beaded creations.

Tiny Holeless Seed Beads

These beads are usually sold in small packages and come in a limited selection of colors. Because they do not have holes, they are used for embellishing a surface through an adhesive.

Bugle Beads

Bugle beads range in size from the standard 4.5mm, which is approximately $\frac{1}{4}$" long, and extend to 25mm, which is approximately 1" long. Bugle beads are made from glass and can be opaque, opaque rainbow, silver-lined, and rainbow ice. Twisted bugle beads add a very dynamic texture to beadwork. Bugle and twisted bugle beads can also be purchased gold-filled or in sterling silver.

Crystal Beads

Crystal beads are clear, brilliant glass beads that are generally manufactured in Austria. They can be either translucent or have an Aurora Borealis finish. The basic bead can have a faceted diamond shape, known as the rondele, or a faceted round shape. Facsimiles of the crystal beads are being manufactured in acrylic.

Fancy Glass Beads

Fancy glass beads are glass beads that have been manufactured in an endless number of shapes, sizes, and colors.

Pearls

Traditional and freshwater pearls can be found in a variety of colors. They are usually sold pre-strung and are relatively inexpensive. The sizes and colors vary within each strand.

Specialty Beads

Specialty beads are also beads that are available in an endless number of shapes, sizes, and colors. They are manufactured in all parts of the world and are made from every kind of natural material and many kinds of synthetic materials.

Wire

Wire is sold in spools of approximately 24 yards. Most of the wire used for this book ranges in size from 32-gauge to 24-gauge, although a few projects require much firmer wire than this. The wire can be purchased as a utilitarian notion, but it is also now available as permanently colored copper wire. The advantage to using the copper wire is that your finished product can be rinsed with water when it needs cleaning without worry that the wire will rust. Permanently colored copper wire is also becoming popular as a decorative element.

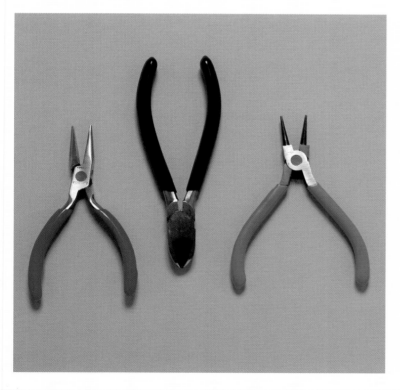

Wire Cutters & Needle-nosed Pliers

These are the only tools required for forming beadwork on wire. Wire cutters are self explanatory and a must for trimming the wire. Needle-nosed pliers come in a variety of shapes, from flat-nosed to round-nosed to bent-nosed. If beadwork is a craft you enjoy, take the time to learn about the specific varieties of cutters and pliers that will enhance your work. Additionally, a bead reamer may be a tool that you find comes in handy. It allows you to enlarge the holes on pearls and other beads.

Forming a Leaf or Flower Petal with a Basic Axis

1. Cut the wire with wire cutters into the required length(s). Tie a knot at one end of each length of wire. The gauge(s) and length(s) of the wire are specified in the materials lists for each project.

2. Slide the specified number and type(s) of beads onto the wire. Position the beads below the knot the number of inches indicated.

3. To proceed with forming the center axis, extend the wire 3" below the bottom bead, then fold the wire back up. Tightly wrap the wire around itself just below the bottom bead. Wire will extend to the left of the basic axis. Grasp the wire and pull it taut with needle-nosed pliers. See Figure 1 on page 11.

4. Smooth the wire so it has a slight bend, beginning where the wire extends at the base of the center axis.

5. Slide the specified number and type(s) of beads onto the wire. Bend the beaded wire to lay snugly next to the left side of the basic axis.

6. Tightly wind the wire around the top bead on the basic axis, taking the wire to the back side of the axis first. The wire will extend to the right of the basic axis. See Figure 2 on page 11.

7. Continue beading each row. Repeat the smoothing and bending process for each row.

8. Make certain to keep the axis straight and straighten the axis after each additional row of beads has been added. See Figure 3 on page 11.

9. Work with the leaf or flower petal from the same facing side with each row and always wrap the wire around the basic axis from the back side to the front side.

10. Repeat Steps 5–7. The eventual leaf or flower petal size is dependant on the number of beaded rows wired to the basic axis.

11. Trim the wires as necessary with wire cutters and tighten the twists with needle-nosed pliers. Be careful to not overtwist as the wire is delicate and will snap. Flatten the cut wire edge against the twists as much as possible with needle-nosed pliers.

12. To determine the front and back sides of the leaf or flower petal, look at both sides. The wire wrappings on one side will be more obvious—this will be the back side.

13. Cut the knot from the tip of the basic axis. Fold the top of the axis wire down to the back side of the leaf or flower petal. Snugly wrap

the wire around the bottom of the axis twice. Cut the looped wire near the base of the axis, straightening the wire to eliminate bulk. Twist the wires and trim.

14. Leaves and flower petals can be formed into a round shape or can be formed into the shapes of leaves or flower petals simply by bending the wires as desired as each row is beaded.

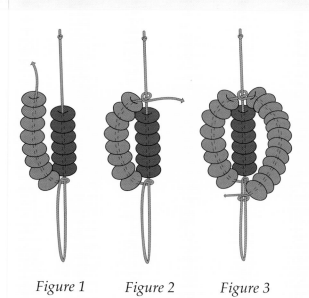

Figure 1   *Figure 2*   *Figure 3*

Making Flower Bud Sprays

1. Cut the 32-gauge wire with wire cutters into the number of 15" lengths needed.

2. Slide the specified number and type(s) of beads onto the wire.

3. Slip the wire around and through the first bead, then tighten the wire so the beads rest snugly against the first bead.

4. Slip the opposite wire around and through the first bead, then tighten the wire.

5. Drape the wires downward against the side of the first bead and twist the wires together. Trim the wires flush about $3\frac{1}{2}$" below the first bead to create a stem.

6. Slide the specified number and type(s) of beads onto both wires.

7. Tie the wires in a knot just below the last bead, then tighten the wire so the beads are snug on the stem.

8. Double stems can be created by separately beading each wire stem. Repeat Steps 6 and 7.

Making Twist Sprays

1. Cut the 32-gauge wire with wire cutters into the number of 15" lengths needed.

2. Slide the specified number and type(s) of beads onto the wire.

3. Bend the wire in half to form a loop. Trim the wires flush about $2\frac{1}{2}$" below the bottom beads to create a stem.

4. Slide the specified number and type(s) of beads onto both wires.

5. Tie the wires in a knot just below the last bead, then tighten the wire so the beads are snug on the stem.

6. Twist the beaded loops as desired.

7. Double stems can be created by separately beading each wire stem. Repeat Steps 5 and 6.

THOUGHTFUL KEEPSAKES

W here do you keep the terra-cotta vase your best friend made for you in pottery class? What place of honor on your Christmas tree is saved for the snowflake ornament made by your best friend? Handcrafted keepsakes bestow sweet thoughts of the recipient as you craft them and tender thoughts of you each time they look at it.

VASES & VIALS

Terra-cotta Mini Vase

Terra-cotta Mini Vase with Saucer, 3" tall

Seed Beads, 11/0:
    Blue Heather, Copper, Mocha,
    Root Beer, Wildberry, 1 container each

Seed Beads, petite: Ginger, 1 container

Seed Beads, tiny holeless: Brown, 1 bag

Mixing Trays

Tacky Craft Glue & Glue Brush

Découpage Medium & Foam Brush

Instructions

1. Wipe the vase and saucer and let dry.

2. Working from the bottom up, daub tacky craft glue around the bottom half of the vase. Smooth the glue with a glue brush, allowing the glue to have an uneven shape near the middle of the vase. Let the glue dry about one minute.

3. Pour all the 11/0 and petite seed beads into a mixing tray to combine all colors.

4. Hold the vase over another mixing tray and pour the bead mixture onto the vase, leaving some areas without beads. Gently press the beads onto the glue.

5. Hold the vase over another mixing tray and pour the tiny holeless seed beads over the entire beaded area, including the areas without beads. Gently press the beads onto the glue. Repeat and let dry.

6. Apply one coat of découpage medium with a foam brush over the entire beaded surface to seal. Let dry.

Wooden Vial

Wooden Vial, $4\frac{1}{2}$" tall

6 Maple Leaves, $\frac{3}{8}$":
    Matte Tourmaline

Seed Beads, 11/0:
    Autumn Heather, Bay Leaf
    Green, Blue Heather, Juniper
    Green, 1 container each

Seed Beads, tiny holeless:
    Apple Green, Black, Brown,
    1 bag each

Mixing Trays

Industrial-strength Adhesive

Tacky Craft Glue & Glue Brush

Découpage Medium & Foam Brush

Adhere the maple leaves evenly around the wooden vial with industrial-strength adhesive. Let the adhesive dry about ten minutes. Using the instructions given for the Terra-cotta Mini Vase on the facing page, proceed gluing on the seed beads in uneven rows of color with the tacky craft glue, making certain to avoid getting glue on the leaves. Seal the beads with one coat of découpage medium.

Porcelain Bud Vase

Porcelain Bud Vase, $4\frac{1}{2}$" tall

Pearls, 2mm:
    Off-white, 1-oz. jar

Seed Beads, tiny holeless:
    Silver, 1 bag

Acrylic Paint: Metallic Gold

Paintbrush

Satin Ribbon, $\frac{1}{8}$"-wide:
    Cream, $\frac{1}{2}$ yard

Mixing Trays

Tacky Craft Glue & Glue Brush

Découpage Medium & Foam Brush

Using the instructions given for the Terra-cotta Mini Vase on pages 14–15, proceed gluing the pearls and the seed beads around the bottom half of the vase with the tacky craft glue. Lightly paint the beaded surface with one coat of metallic gold paint and let dry. Seal the pearls and the beads with one coat of découpage medium. Tie a piece of satin ribbon into a bow around the neck of the vase.

Elastic Cord, 8mm

Seed Beads, 11/0:
   Any Color or
   Combination of Colors,
   approximately 115 beads
   for each bracelet

Silver Crimp Tube, $\frac{1}{8}$"-long:
   1 for each bracelet

Needle-nosed Pliers

BRACELETS

Instructions

1.   Cut the elastic cord into one 15" length for each bracelet.

2.   Thread the seed beads in the color(s) desired onto each length of elastic.

3.   Slide a crimp tube onto one end of each length of elastic.

4.   Using a sailor's knot (left over right, then right over left), tie the ends of each length of elastic together. Trim the ends of the elastic fairly short.

5.   Slide the crimp tube over the knot and crimp in place with needle-nosed pliers.

SNOWFLAKES

Snowflake Ornaments

An Assortment of Beads:
> Any Size and Color or
> Combination of Sizes
> and Colors

18-gauge Wire

Wire Cutters

Flux

Soldering Iron & Solder

Needle-nosed Pliers

Instructions

1. Cut the wire with wire cutters into four equal lengths for each snowflake ornament. Arrange the wires into a snowflake shape.

2. Apply a small amount of flux to the center of the wires where they intersect and solder together with a soldering iron.

3. Thread beads onto the snowflake as desired.

4. Curl each wire end with needle-nosed pliers.

LILY OF THE VALLEY

Lily of the Valley Bouquet with Heart Sprays

Seed Beads, 11/0:
   Bay Leaf Green, Pearl, Vanilla,
   1 container each

Seed Beads, tiny holeless: Clear, 1 bag

Bugle Beads, small:
   Crystal, Mauve, 1 container each

14 Pearls, 4mm: Ivory

38 Pearls, 6mm: Ivory

9 Heart-shaped Beads, 6mm:
   Frosted Clear

26-gauge Wire: Flesh

32-gauge Wire: Silver

12 Velvet Leaves, 1" x 1½":
   Beige/Light Green

Sheer Ribbon, 1½"-wide:
   Ivory/Gold, ¾ yard

Florist Tape

Mixing Tray

Tacky Craft Glue & Glue Brush

Découpage Medium & Foam Brush

Wire Cutters

Pinking Shears

Instructions

To Make the Lily of the Valley Sprays:

1.   Cut the 26-gauge wire with wire cutters into eight 15" lengths. Tie a knot at one end of each length of wire.

2.   Slide seven 6mm pearls and two 4mm pearls onto one of the lengths of wire to make the first spray. Move the pearls to the center of the wire.

3.   Slide five vanilla and five pearl seed beads onto the wire and bend the wire to form a loop from the seed beads. Twist the wires together just below the bottom of the seed beads. Slide the pearl closest to the loop toward the twists in the wire and pull the wires taut. See the illustration below.

4.   Alternating colors, slide five vanilla and pearl seed beads onto the free wire. Bend the wire around the first pearl in the chain and wrap it around the wire with the pearls, just below the first pearl, to anchor it. Pull the wires taut. The

seed beads will encircle half of the pearl. Repeat with another five seed beads, this time encircling the next pearl on the opposite side, creating an "S" curve or serpentine around the pearls. See the illustration below.

5. Continue to serpentine the seed beads around the pearls. Twist the wires together below the last pearl and slide one mauve bugle bead onto both of the wires.

6. Separate the wires and slide two bay leaf green seed beads and and one mauve bugle bead onto each wire. Repeat this sequence of beads for a total of six combinations on each wire and twist the wires together below the last bugle beads. Twist the two beaded wires together to make a twisted stem on the lily of the valley spray.

7. Repeat Steps 2–6 to make additional lily of the valley sprays. Make an additional two sprays with seven 6mm and two 4mm pearls; two sprays with five 6mm and two 4mm pearls; one spray with three 6mm and two 4mm pearls; and two sprays with two 6mm and one 4mm pearls (8 sprays are needed). Use fewer bay leaf green seed beads and mauve bugle beads to make the stems for the shorter lily of the valley sprays.

To Make the Heart Sprays:

1. Cut the 32-gauge wire with wire cutters into nine 10" lengths.

2. Slide one heart-shaped and two pearl seed beads onto one of the lengths of wire to make the first spray. Move the beads to the center of the wire.

3. Bend the wire in half and slide the wire around the top seed bead and through the second seed and heart-shaped beads. Adjust and trim the wires so they are even. See the illustration below.

4. Slide one bay leaf green seed and one crystal bugle beads onto both wires. Repeat this sequence of beads for a total of nine combinations and twist the wires together below the last bugle bead to make a stem on the heart spray.

5. Repeat Steps 2–4 to make additional heart sprays (9 sprays are needed). Use fewer bay leaf green seed and crystal bugle beads to make the stems for some shorter heart sprays.

To Make the Lily of the Valley and Heart Sprays Bouquet and Frosted Velvet Leaves:

1.   Arrange the lily of the valley and heart sprays and twist the wires together.

2.   Glue the top edge of one velvet leaf onto the bottom edge of another velvet leaf, over-lapping the leaves about $\frac{1}{2}$". Repeat until you have six velvet leaves made from twelve velvet leaves.

3.   Trim the leaves into long, narrow leaves with pinking shears.

4.   Daub tacky craft glue over the velvet side of each leaf. Smooth the glue with a glue brush. Let the glue dry about one minute.

5.   Hold each leaf over a mixing tray and pour the tiny holeless seed beads onto the leaves to frost. Gently press the beads onto the glue and let dry.

6.   Apply one coat of découpage medium with a foam brush over each frosted leaf to seal. Let dry.

7.   Wire the frosted velvet leaves onto the lily of the valley and heart sprays and trim the wires.

8.   Wrap the twisted wires with florist tape for a finished look and tie a piece of sheer ribbon into a bow around the bouquet.

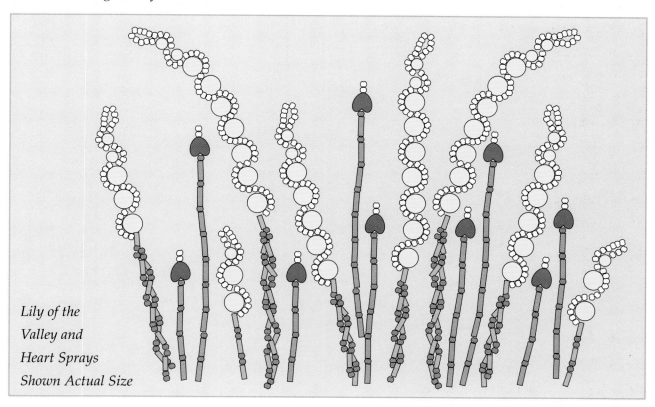

Lily of the Valley and Heart Sprays Shown Actual Size

TREASURE CHESTS

Hexagon Boxes

2 Papier Mâché Boxes, 3"

Acrylic Paint: Metallic Silver

Paintbrush

Seed Beads, 11/0: Cream, Ice,
    White, 1 container each

Freshwater Pearls, small: White

6 Various Star Charms

Beading Thread

Mixing Tray

Tacky Craft Glue & Glue Brush

Découpage Medium & Foam Brush

Paint the boxes with metallic silver paint and let dry. Using the instructions given for the Terra-cotta Mini Vase on pages 14–15, combine the cream, ice, and white seed beads. Proceed gluing the seed beads around the bottom of one box with the tacky craft glue. Glue the seed beads in a star shape on top of the lid for the other box. String one freshwater pearl, two ice, three cream, and two ice seed beads onto a length of beading thread. Repeat this sequence of beads until you have enough to meander around the sides of the box with the beaded bottom. Adhere in place as desired with tacky craft glue. Randomly glue one star charm to each side of the box. Seal the pearls and the beads with one coat of découpage medium.

$\mathcal{P}$in-beaded Fruit

Variety of Plastic Fruit

Seed Beads, 11/0:
  Clear, 1 container

Sequins, Metallic Colors
  to Match the Natural Colors
  of the Fruit

Straight Pins, $\frac{3}{4}$"

F R U I T

Instructions

1. Place one seed bead and one metallic-colored sequin onto each straight pin.

2. Beginning at the top of each piece of plastic fruit, push the pins into the plastic. Overlap as necessary to completely cover the fruit.

MULTIFACETED SPARKLE

There are those things you love so much that you find a use for them wherever you can. Your mother's amethyst hatpin adorns your cozy wool coat. That beautiful vase of flowers, adorned with a beaded cluster of grapes, calls attention to your dining table. With a bit of creativity, one pretty piece can delight in so many unexpected ways.

PINS

methyst Heart Pin

Seed Beads, 11/0: Orchid, 1 container

Bugle Beads, small: Mauve, 1 container

Round Crystal Beads, 4mm:
  Amethyst, 3 containers

1 Specialty Bead, 12mm x 8mm Oval:
  Lavender

24-gauge Wire: Silver

32-gauge Wire: Silver

Pin Back, 1": Silver

Wire Cutters

Needle-nosed Pliers

Instructions

1.   Cut the 24-gauge wire with wire cutters into one 36" length. Tie a knot at one end of the length of wire.

2.   Refer to the General Instructions for Forming a Leaf or Flower Petal with a Basic Axis on pages 10–11. Slide two seed beads, the specialty bead, and two seed beads onto the wire. Position the beads 4" below the knot. Proceed with forming the center axis.

3.   Row 1: Alternate and slide five seed and four round crystal beads onto the wire. Anchor the wire to the upper end of the axis wire. Repeat for second half of Row 1.

4. Continue to form rows around the center axis as follows:

Row 2: Bugle, seed, bugle, seed, bugle, seed, round crystal, seed, round crystal, seed, round crystal, seed. Repeat for second half of Row 2.

Row 3: Seed, bugle, seed, bugle, seed, bugle, three seeds, round crystal, seed, round crystal, seed, round crystal, three seeds. Repeat for second half of Row 3. Begin to mold the wire into a heart shape.

Row 4: Three seeds, bugle, seed, bugle, seed, bugle, seed, round crystal, seed, round crystal, seed, round crystal, seed, round crystal, seed, round crystal, two seeds. Repeat for second half of Row 4.

Row 5: Four seeds, bugle, seed, bugle, seed, bugle, seed, round crystal, seed, round crystal, seed, round crystal, seed, round crystal, seed, round crystal, seed, round crystal, three seeds. Repeat for second half of Row 5.

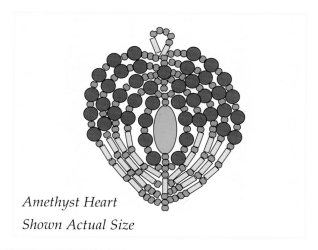

Amethyst Heart
Shown Actual Size

5. After anchoring the second half of Row 5 onto the axis wire, cut one side of the looped axis wire about $\frac{1}{2}$" from the tip of the heart. Bend this wire underneath the heart and flatten. Bend the long wire upward. Slide three seed, one bugle, and two seed beads onto this wire. Move the beads so they fit snugly against the tip of the heart. Position the wire over the bottom center of the heart so the beads cover the center axis wires.

6. Slip the wire to the back side of the heart just above the bottom of the first beaded row. Secure the wire to the back side of the heart by invisibly wrapping it around the bottom portion of the center axis. Trim the wires, then flatten with needle-nosed pliers.

7. Trim the knot off the remaining length of wire at the top of the heart. Slide one bugle, five seed, one bugle bead, two seed, one round crystal, and two seed beads onto this wire. Move the beads so they fit snugly against the top of the heart.

8. Bend the beaded wire to form a small loop and twist. Secure the excess wire to the back side of the top of the heart by invisibly wrapping it around the upper portion of the center axis. Trim the wires, then flatten with needle-nosed pliers.

9. Cut the 32-gauge wire into one 15" length. Invisibly wire the pin back to the back of the heart.

Fan-shaped Pin

Seed Beads, 11/0:
   Silver, 1 container

32 Seed Beads, petite: Silver

15 Round Crystal Beads,
   4mm: Black Aurora Borealis

49 Rondele Crystal Beads,
   4mm: Black Aurora Borealis

2 Specialty Beads,
   5mm x 3mm Oval:
   Hemalyke

3 Teardrop-shaped Beads,
   8mm x 4mm: Black

24-gauge Wire: Silver

32-gauge Wire: Silver

Pin Back, 1": Silver

Wire Cutters

Needle-nosed Pliers

Instructions

To Form the Fan Shape:

1.   Cut the 24-gauge wire with wire cutters into one 30" length.

2.   Slide one 11/0 seed, 17 rondele crystal, and one 11/0 seed beads onto the wire. Move the beads to the center of the wire. Bend the beaded wire into a semicircle. At the seed beads, bend the wire inward from each side.

3.   Alternating colors, slide five rondele crystal beads onto each end of the wire.

Twist the ends of the wire together where the five crystal beads from each side meet in the middle. Straighten the beaded wire at the bottom of the semicircle to form a straight edge.

4. The wire on the beaded semicircle will be the anchor wire.

To Fill the Fan Shape:

1. Cut the 32-gauge wire with wire cutters into one 40" length. Bend the wire in half and attach this length of wire to the anchor wire at the middle of the straight edge.

2. Slide two 11/0 seed and six rondele crystal beads onto one end of the wire.

3. Extend the beaded wire to the top of the fan shape and wrap the wire around the anchor wire in between the second and third crystal beads from the center. Slip the wire back through the crystal beads. Wrap the wire around the straight edge of the anchor wire, then tightly drape the wire along the back side to the next adjacent space between beads.

4. Slide one 11/0 seed, four round crystal, and one 11/0 seed beads onto the same wire.

5. Repeat Step 3, wrapping the wire around the fourth and fifth crystal beads from the center.

6. Slide one 11/0 seed, three rondele crystal, and one 11/0 seed beads onto the same wire.

7. Repeat Step 3, wrapping the wire around the sixth and seventh crystal beads from the center.

8. Slide one 11/0 seed, one round crystal, and one 11/0 seed beads onto the same wire.

9. Repeat Step 3, wrapping the wire around the seventh and eighth crystal beads from the center. The wire should then be tightly draped along the back side so it can be wrapped in between the 11/0 seed bead and the eighth crystal bead from the center. Do not trim the wire.

10. Repeat Steps 2–9 for the remaining end of the 32-gauge wire, filling the other side of the fan shape.

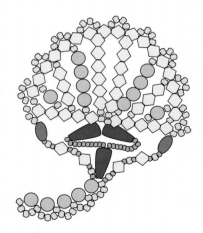

Fan-shaped Pin
Shown Actual Size

To Scallop the Beads Around the Fan Shape:

1.   Using the 32-gauge wire at the right side of the fan shape, slide four 11/0 seed beads onto the wire.

2.   Slip the beads down the wire so they "scallop" snugly around the outer side of the eighth crystal bead. Wrap the wire around the anchor wire twice.

3.   Tightly drape the wire along the back side so it can be wrapped in between the seventh and sixth crystal beads from the center.

4.   Slide four 11/0 seed beads onto the wire.

5.   Repeat Step 2, scalloping the beads around the outer side of the sixth crystal bead.

6.   Tightly drape the wire along the back side so it can be wrapped in between the fifth and fourth crystal beads from the center.

7.   Continue to scallop the beads around the semicircle of the fan shape in the same manner as in Steps 1–6. Do not trim the wire.

To Form the Handle:

1.   Separate the 24-gauge wires that extend down from the straight edge of the fan shape. Slide one teardrop-shaped and ten petite seed beads onto each wire. Bend the wires to form the inner triangle shape of the handle. Tightly twist the wires together, then slide the third teardrop-shaped bead through both wires.

2.   Allow one of the wires to be bent to the left of the last teardrop-shaped bead, with the other wire pointing downward.

3.   For the handle of the fan, slide five round crystal beads onto the wire pointing downward. Push the beads upward to meet the teardrop-shaped bead. Slide five 11/0 seed beads onto the wire. Move the beads along the wire so they scallop snugly around the right side of the crystal bead that is on the bottom. Wrap the wire around the handle anchor wire once.

4.   Continue to scallop the beads around the remaining crystal beads in the same manner as in Step 3, using four 11/0 seed beads for each scallop.

5.   When the scalloping is complete there will be a wire extending from both sides of the teardrop-shaped bead. Working with the wire on the right side, slide beads onto the wire in the following order: petite seed, 11/0 seed, petite seed, rondele crystal, petite seed, 11/0 seed, petite seed, rondele crystal, petite seed, 11/0 seed, petite seed, specialty, three 11/0 seed beads. Bend the wire and wrap it over the straight edge of the fan shape at the outer right crystal bead. Repeat for the wire on the left side.

6.   Slide four more 11/0 seed beads onto the wire on the right side. Bend the wire to form a very small loop, making certain the wire can lay straight along the back side of the straight edge of the fan shape (these beads will not show). Repeat for the wire on the left side.

7.   Using the remaining 32-gauge wire, invisibly wire the pin back to the back of the fan shape along the straight edge.

8.   While wiring on the pin back, secure the 24-gauge wire. When secure, trim the wire $\frac{1}{4}$" past the last seed bead. Continue to use the 32-gauge wire to secure the pin back in place, then trim. Flatten with needle-nosed pliers, then tuck the wire ends away.

Petite Butterfly Pin

Seed Beads, 11/0:
   Royal Blue, Sea Blue, 1 container each

2 Cube-shaped Beads, 6mm x 8mm: Aqua

2 Twisted Beads, 4mm x 8mm: Turquoise

Round Beads, 6mm:
   1 Dark Blue, 1 Frosted Lavender

1 Teardrop-shaped Bead, 12mm x 6mm: Blue

26-gauge Wire: Green

32-gauge Wire: Green

Pin Back, 1": Silver

Wire Cutters

Needle-nosed Pliers

This petite butterfly can also be wired onto a variety of hair accessories, included in a floral bouquet, or used to embellish a simple pillow. Look to Mother Nature for inspiration when selecting colors for your creation!

Instructions

To Form the Upper Wings:

1. Cut the 26-gauge wire with wire cutters into two 36" lengths. Tie a knot at one end of each length of wire.

2. Refer to the General Instructions for Forming a Leaf or Flower Petal with a Basic Axis on pages 10–11. Slide one cube-shaped bead onto one of the lengths of wire, positioning the bead 4" below the knot. Extend the wire 3" below the bottom of the bead and proceed with forming the center axis.

3. Alternating colors, form one beaded row of seed beads and wrap it around the center axis. Slide the wire back through the cube-shaped bead. There will now be two wires extending from the upper end of the wing—one has a knot in one end. Bend one wire to the left and one wire to the right of the cube-shaped bead. Trim the knot with wire cutters from the one wire.

4. Alternating colors, form one beaded row of seed beads onto the wire on the left and wrap it around the center axis. Repeat for the wire on the right.

5. Repeat Steps 2–4 with the remaining length of wire to form the second upper wing.

6. Twist the two upper wings together. Tighten the twists with needle-nosed pliers.

Petite Butterfly
Shown Actual Size

To Form the Lower Wings:

1. Bend the double wires upward. Bend the two short wires upward. Bend the long wires downward so they extend to the left and right of each other.

2. Slide one twisted bead onto the wire on the left. Move the bead close to where the upper wings have been joined. Extend the wire 3" below the twisted bead, then fold the wire back up to form a loop. Slide the wire back through the twisted bead, allowing the 3" loop to remain. Twist the loop wires together just below the twisted bead.

3. Cut the loop apart with wire cutters. Alternating colors, slide seed beads onto one of the wires. Bend the wire around the twisted bead and snugly wrap the wire at the top of the twisted bead, as if onto an axis wire. Repeat for the remaining wire.

4. On the back side, twist the two wires together and bend them upward.

5. Repeat Steps 2–4 for the wire on the right.

To Form the Body of the Butterfly:

1. Cut the loop wire so one end is long and one end is short. There will now be four longer wires among the short wires. Twist all the short wires together. Tighten the twists with needle-nosed pliers. Trim the wires, then flatten with needle-nosed pliers.

2. Bend two of the longer wires upward and to the back side of the butterfly center. Twist these two wires together. Slide two round, one teardrop-shaped, and one seed beads onto both wires. Bend the wires over the front side to make the body and then bend the wires back underneath the butterfly. The remaining amount of these wires can be used to wire the pin back onto the back side of the butterfly.

*Petite Butterfly
Shown Actual Size*

To Form the Antennae:

1. Slide two seed beads onto one of the remaining wires. Coil the wire end about $\frac{3}{4}$" from the head of the butterfly with needle-nosed pliers. Trim the wire close to the coil, then flatten with needle-nosed pliers.

2. Repeat Step 1 for the remaining wire.

3. Cut the 32-gauge wire into one 15" length. Invisibly wire the pin back to the back of the butterfly.

This petite butterfly pin has been transformed into a stick pin that will grace any lapel or hat.

ORNAMENT

oravian Star

Papier Mâché Star, $3\frac{1}{2}$"

Acrylic Paint: Metallic Purple

Paintbrush

Premixed Seed/Bugle Beads:
  Crystal Pearl, 1-oz. jar

Seed Beads, tiny holeless: Lavender, 1 bag

Accent Beads, 4mm–6mm:
  Assorted Pearls and Crystals,
  approximately 35

Iridescent Glue, 1.25-oz. bottle

Straight Pins, $1\frac{1}{6}$"

Mixing Trays

Tacky Craft Glue & Glue Brush

Instructions

1. Paint the star with one coat of metallic purple paint and let dry.

2. Working with the upper portion of the star, daub tacky craft glue onto one side of each star point. Smooth the glue with a glue brush. Let the glue dry about one minute.

3. Hold the star over a mixing tray and pour the premixed seed/bugle beads onto the star. Gently press the beads onto the glue.

4. Hold the star over another mixing tray and pour the tiny holeless seed beads over the entire beaded area. Gently press the beads onto the glue. Repeat and let dry.

5. Repeat Step 2 for the bottom portion of the star. Repeat Steps 3 and 4 until the entire star has been beaded.

6. Paint a thin layer of iridesent glue over the entire beaded areas with a glue brush and let dry.

7. Slide one 4mm or 6mm pearl or crystal onto a straight pin. Daub tacky craft glue onto the straight pin just below the bead. Push the straight pin into the star at a point. Randomly using 4mm and 6mm pearls and crystals, repeat until each star point and inner angle corner has a bead.

Velvet Eggplant

Velvet Eggplant Pincushion, approximately 4" x 8"

Seed Beads, 11/0:
Frosted Autumn, Jade, Light Crimson, Orange, Yellow-Green, 1 container each

Bugle Beads, small:
Christmas Green, 1 container

Beading Pins, 1 $\frac{1}{6}$"

PINCUSHION

Instructions

1. Working with one bead at a time, slide each bead onto a straight pin and arrange as follows: To make the carrots, use the orange and frosted autumn seed beads; to make the carrot tops, use the jade and yellow-green seed beads; to make leaves, use one or two Christmas green bugle beads. Add some light crimson and orange seed beads and a few bugle beads onto the front of the eggplant as desired.

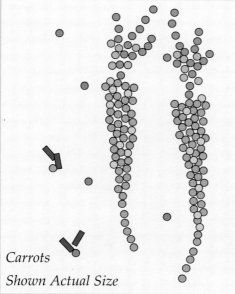

Carrots
Shown Actual Size

KEEPSAKE KEEPER

Pansy Lid on Goblet

Green Goblet or Wine Glass, 5 $\frac{1}{2}$" tall

Seed Beads, 11/0:
  Christmas Green, Crystal Lilac, Crystal
  Mint, Frosted Lilac, Frosted Royal Purple,
  Ice, Light Green, Lilac Ice, Periwinkle,
  Satin Blue, Violet, 1 container each

Bugle Beads, small:
  Crystal, Willow, 1 container each

3 Round Beads, 4mm: Crystal

2 Round Beads, 6mm: Frosted Blue

3 Rice-shaped Beads, 5mm: Dark Purple

26-gauge Wire: Silver

32-gauge Wire: Silver

8 Velvet Leaves, 1" x 1 $\frac{1}{2}$":
  Lavender/Light Green

Velvet Scraps: Pale Green

Needle & Thread

Heavy-weight Cardboard

Industrial-strength Adhesive

Measuring Tape

Scissors

Wire Cutters

Needle-nosed Pliers

Instructions

To Make the Pansy Petals:

1. Cut the 26-gauge wire with wire cutters into five 30" lengths. Tie a knot at one end of each length of wire.

2. Refer to the General Instructions for Forming a Leaf or Flower Petal with a Basic Axis on pages 10–11. Slide one 6mm round bead onto one of the lengths of wire, positioning the bead 2" below the knot. Proceed with forming the center axis.

3. Alternating shades of lilac (lavender), form five rows of seed beads and wrap them around the center axis.

4. Repeat Steps 2 and 3 to make one more lavender petal (2 petals are needed).

5. Slide one rice-shaped and two violet seed beads onto one of the lengths of wire, positioning the beads 2" below the knot. Proceed with forming the center axis.

6. Alternating shades of purple, form four rows of seed beads and wrap them around the center axis. Using ice seed beads, form one more beaded row and wrap it around the last row of purple seed beads.

7. Repeat Steps 5 and 6 to make one more purple/ice petal (2 petals are needed).

8. Repeat Steps 5 and 6 to make one more purple/ice petal, forming one additional row of ice seed beads so this petal is one row larger than the previous two purple/ice petals.

9. Cut the 26-gauge wire into one 12" length. Tie a knot at one end of the length of wire.

10. Slide three ice seed beads onto the wire, positioning the beads 2" below the knot. Proceed with forming the center axis.

11. Using ice seed beads, form two rows of ice seed beads and wrap them around the center axis.

12. Arrange the two smallest purple/ice petals next to each other and twist the wires together. Center the larger purple/ice petal

All Shown Actual Size

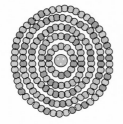

Lavender Petal

Purple/Ice Petal

Purple/Ice Petal with Additional Row of Ice Seed Beads

Small Ice Petal (Center)

over the two joined purple/ice petals and twist the wires together. Arrange the two lavender petals next to each other and twist the wires together. Center the two joined lavender petals behind the three joined purple/ice petals and twist the wires together. Slip the small ice petal through the center of the five pansy petals and twist the wires together. Tighten the twists with needle-nosed pliers.

13. Trim the wires with wire cutters to $1\frac{1}{2}$" length on the back side of the pansy.

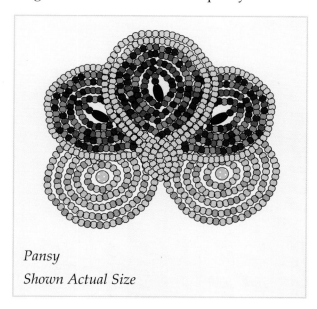

Pansy
Shown Actual Size

To Make the Flower Bud and Twist Sprays and To Finish the Lid on the Goblet:

1. Refer to the General Instructions for Making Flower Bud Sprays on page 11. Use one 4mm round and four satin blue seed beads for each flower bud spray (3 sprays are needed). Alternating colors, slide crystal bugle and satin blue seed beads onto the 32-gauge wire stem.

2. Refer to the General Instructions for Making Twist Sprays on page 11. Use a combination of crystal mint and light green seed beads for one twist spray and a combination of Christmas green and light green seed beads for the other twist spray (2 sprays are needed). Slide five willow bugle beads onto the 32-gauge wire stem.

3. Measure the opening of the goblet and cut one cardboard circle with scissors $\frac{1}{8}$" smaller than the opening. Cover the cardboard with a scrap of velvet to make the lid and gather it at the top with a needle and thread.

4. Position the pansy on top of the velvet lid and tightly hand-stitch the stem to the velvet encased cardboard.

5. Glue three velvet leaves underneath the pansy with industrial-strength adhesive.

6. Arrange the three flower bud sprays and the two twist sprays randomly around the stem of the goblet and wire in place. Glue two velvet leaves around the stem of the goblet to hide the wires. Glue the three remaining velvet leaves around the base of the goblet.

PILLOW

Champagne-colored Fringe on Floral Pillow

Light Pink Pillow, small

Seed Beads, 11/0:

Bay Leaf Green, Crystal Mint, Crystal Pink, Frosted Mauve, Frosted Pink, Frosted Pink Parfait, Frosted Rose, Lemon Lime, Pink, 1 container each

Champagne, 500 per repeat on fringe

3 Round Beads, 8mm: Frosted White

Glass Beads, 6mm:

Clear, 24 per repeat on fringe

Glass Beads, 8mm:

Clear Rose Quartz, 2 per repeat on fringe

Satin Ribbon, 1 $\frac{1}{4}$"-wide:

Light Pink

Twill Tape, $\frac{3}{8}$"-wide

26-gauge Wire: Gold

Needle & Beading Thread

Wire Cutters

Needle-nosed Pliers

Instructions

To Make the Flowers:

1. Cut the 26-gauge wire with wire cutters into thirteen 30" lengths. Tie a knot at one end of each length of wire.

2. Refer to the General Instructions for Forming a Leaf or Flower Petal with a Basic Axis on pages 10–11. Slide four assorted pink seed beads onto one of the lengths of wire, positioning the bead 2" below the knot. Proceed with forming the center axis.

3. Alternating shades of pink, form four rows of seed beads and wrap them around the center axis.

4. Repeat Steps 2 and 3 to make twelve more pink petals (13 petals are needed).

5.   Arrange five petals to make a single flower and twist the wires together on the back side of the flower. Repeat to make one more five-petal flower and make one three-petal flower.

6.   Cut the 26-gauge wire into three 8" lengths. Slide one 8mm round bead onto each length of wire. Move the beads to the center of the wires. Bend each wire in half and slide both wire ends through the centers of the flowers. Twist the wires together.

Flower
Shown Actual Size

To Make the Leaves:

1.   Cut the 26-gauge wire with wire cutters into eight 20" lengths. Tie a knot at one end of each length of wire.

2.   Refer to the General Instructions for Forming a Leaf or Flower Petal with a Basic Axis on pages 10–11. Slide four assorted green seed beads onto one of the lengths of wire, positioning the bead 2" below the knot. Proceed with forming the center axis.

3.   Alternating shades of green, form three rows of seed beads and wrap them around the center axis.

4.   Repeat Steps 2 and 3 to make seven more green leaves (8 leaves are needed). Finish the first inch of wire with ribbon.

5.   Arrange three leaves and twist the wires together. Repeat to make one more three-leaf cluster.

6.   Add one three-leaf cluster onto a five-petal flower and twist the wires together. Add the remaining three-leaf cluster onto the three-petal flower and twist the wires together. Trim the wires with wire cutters 4" below the back side of the flowers and finish the wires with ribbon.

7.   Trim the wires on the two remaining leaves $3\frac{1}{4}$" below the bottom of the leaves. Finish the wires with ribbon. Hand-stitch assorted green seed beads randomly onto the ribbon on the top side of the stems.

To Make the Fringe:

Note: There are six rows of beads in each repeat.

1. Knot the thread onto the edge of twill tape 1" from the end with a needle and double strand of beading thread.

2. Row 1: Slide four seed, one 6mm glass, 46 seed, one 6mm glass, two seed, one 6mm glass, two seed, one 6mm glass, and one seed beads onto the beading thread.

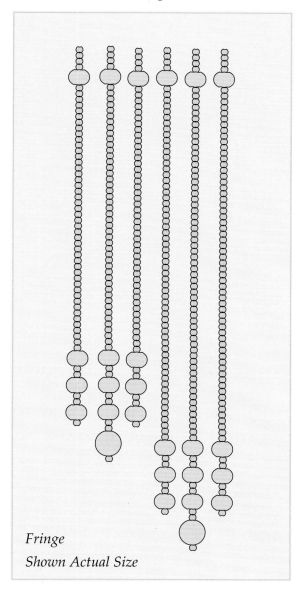

Fringe
Shown Actual Size

3. Slide the thread back through all of the beads, except the last seed bead. Secure the beaded strand to the twill tape. Stitch the beading thread $\frac{1}{4}$" from the first row through the twill tape.

4. Row 2: Slide four seed, one 6mm glass, 46 seed, one 6mm glass, two seed, one 6mm glass, two seed, one 6mm glass, two seed, one 8mm glass, and one seed beads onto the beading thread. Repeat Step 3.

5. Row 3: Repeat Steps 2 and 3.

6. Row 4: Repeat Step 2, using 61 seed beads instead of 46. Repeat Step 3.

7. Row 5: Repeat Step 4, using 61 seed beads instead of 46. Repeat Step 3.

8. Row 6: Repeat Step 2, using 61 seed beads instead of 46. Repeat Step 3.

9. Continue the repeat until you have two 8" lengths of fringe.

To Attach the Flowers and the Fringe to the Pillow:

1. Arrange and hand-stitch the flower stems onto the pillow as desired.

2. Stitch the twill tape with the fringe to both sides of the pillow, making certain to turn the twill tape under at the top and bottom edges.

3. Hand-stitch ribbon along the edges of the pillow to cover the twill tape.

CENTERPIECE

Vase Embellished with Grape Clusters & Margarita Bouquet

Glass Vase, 8" tall

Seed Beads, 11/0:
Christmas Green, Light Green,
1 container each

Bugle Beads, small:
Peppermint, 1 container

42 Round Beads, 3mm:
Mother of Pearl

6 Round Beads, 4mm:
Light Mauve Freshwater Pearl

34 Round Beads, 8mm: Jade

24 Acrylic Round Crystal Drop
Beads, 20mm: Amethyst

24-gauge Wire: Silver

26-gauge Wire: Flesh

32-gauge Wire: Silver

3 Velvet Leaves, 1" x 1 $\frac{1}{2}$":
Lavender/Light Green

Silk Leaves, 1" x 1 $\frac{1}{2}$": Gold/Green

Wire-edged Ribbon, 1"-wide:
Mauve Cross-dyed, $\frac{3}{4}$ yard

Florist Tape

Wire Cutters

Instructions

To Make the Green Grape Sprays (Cluster):

1.   Cut the 26-gauge wire with wire cutters into eight 10" lengths.

2.   Slide five 8mm round and one light green seed beads onto one of the lengths of wire to make the first spray. Move the beads to the center of the wire. Bend one wire end around the seed bead, then back through the five round beads. Twist the wires together below the bottom beads.

3.   Repeat Step 2, making one more spray with five round beads, three sprays with four round beads, and two sprays with three round beads (7 sprays are needed).

4.   Wire the remaining six 8mm round beads individually into a ball.

5.   Arrange the seven green sprays together with the individually wired beads at the top and twist the wires together to make the green grape cluster.

To Make the Purple Grape Cluster:

1.   Cut the 24-gauge wire with wire cutters into one 20" length.

2.   Slide one round crystal drop bead onto the length of wire to make the first spray. Move the bead to the center of the wire.

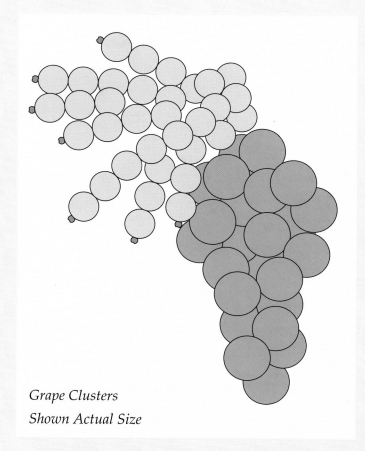

Grape Clusters
Shown Actual Size

Twist the wires together. Bend one wire end to the left and one to the right.

3.   Slide one round crystal drop bead onto each wire. With the wired sides of the beads facing each other, twist the wires together. Position the beads below the top bead and to the left and right of the center bead. Bend one wire end to the left and one to the right. Slide one round crystal drop bead onto each wire. Position the beads so they rest upon and are opposite the previous two beads. Twist the wires together.

4. Continue adding two beads at a time, each time alternating the position of the beads, for a total of seven sets.

5. Cut the 24-gauge wire into three 10" lengths.

6. Repeat Steps 1–3 for each length of wire, making three groups with three beads each.

7. Arrange the three groups of beads together at the top of the previous group of beads and twist the wires together to make the purple grape cluster.

To Make the Margarita Sprays:

1. Refer to the instructions for making the Margarita Sprays on page 99. Use seven 3mm round and one 4mm round beads for

each margarita spray. Slide four or five green seed and one bugle beads onto the 32-gauge wire stem. Then slide two green seed and one bugle beads onto the wire, repeating this sequence of beads for a total of two to four combinations and twist the wires together below the last bugle bead.

2. Repeat Step 1 to make additional margarita sprays (6 sprays are needed). Use fewer green seed beads to make the stems for some shorter margarita sprays. Make three sprays with Christmas green stems and three sprays with light green stems.

To Make the Grape Clusters and Margarita Sprays Bouquet:

1. Cut the 24-gauge wire with wire cutters into one 24" length.

2. Bend the wire in half and twist to create a form. Arrange the grape clusters and margarita sprays on the form and wire in place.

3. Wire the velvet and silk leaves at the top of the arrangement and trim the wires with wire cutters.

4. Wrap the twisted wires with florist tape for a finished look and tie a piece of wire-edged ribbon into a bow around the bouquet. Attach the grape cluster and margarita spray bouquet around the neck of the vase.

RIBBON-WRAPPED WREATH

rosted Leaf
Oval Wreath

Seed Beads, 11/0:
  Champagne Ice, Coral Ice, Ice,
  Light Pink, 1 container each

32 Rondele Crystal Beads, 6mm: Clear

4 Amethyst Rocks, small: Amethyst

12 Frosted Leaves, 18mm:
  Rose Quartz

26-gauge Wire: Flesh

Silver Metal Ring, 5"-diameter

Silk Ribbon, 4mm: Blush, 4 yards

Wire Cutters

Needle-nosed Pliers

Instructions

To Make the Flower Petals:

1.   Cut the 26-gauge wire with wire cutters into two 30" lengths. Tie a knot at one end of each length of wire.

2.   Refer to the General Instructions for Forming a Leaf or Flower Petal with a Basic Axis on pages 10–11. Slide four champagne ice seed beads onto one of the lengths of wire, positioning the beads 2" below the knot. Proceed with forming the center axis.

3.   Form five rows of seed beads and wrap them around the center axis. Use champagne ice for the first row, ice for the second row, champagne ice for the third row, alternating two coral ice and one ice for the fourth row, and two coral ice and one light pink for the fifth row.

4.   Repeat Steps 2 and 3 to make one more petal (2 petals are needed).

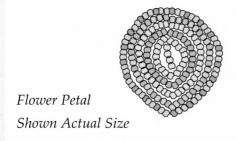

Flower Petal

Shown Actual Size

To Make the Frosted Leaf Sprays:

1.   Cut the 26-gauge wire with wire cutters into twelve 10" lengths.

2.   Slide one frosted leaf and five seed beads onto one of the lengths of wire. Move the beads to the center of the wire. Bend one wire end around the seed beads, then back through the frosted leaf. Twist the wires together below the leaf.

3.   Arrange the two flower petals next to each other and twist the wires together. Center the frosted leaf spray at the bottom of the two joined flower petals and twist the wires together.

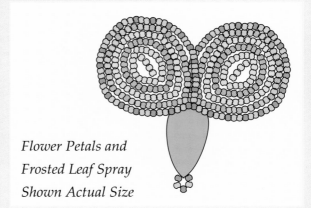

Flower Petals and

Frosted Leaf Spray

Shown Actual Size

4.   Slide eight light pink seed, one crystal, two ice seed, one crystal, two light pink seed beads, one frosted leaf, and five seed beads onto one of the lengths of wire. Move the beads to the center of the wire. Bend one wire end around the seed beads, then back through the frosted leaf. Twist the wires together below the last seed bead.

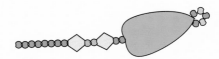

Frosted Leaf Spray

Shown Actual Size

5. Repeat Step 4 to make ten more frosted leaf sprays (11 sprays are needed).

To Make the Amethyst Rock Sprays:

1. Cut the 26-gauge wire with wire cutters into two 8" lengths.

2. Slide five seed beads, one amethyst rock, one crystal bead, one amethyst rock, and three seed beads onto one of the lengths of wire.

3. Move the beads to the center of the wire. Bend one wire end around the seed beads, then back through the rocks and beads. Twist the wires together below the last seed bead.

4. Slide one seed bead, one amethyst rock, one crystal bead, one amethyst rock, and three seed beads onto the remaining length of wire. Repeat Step 3 to make one more amethyst rock spray.

*Amethyst Rock Sprays
Shown Actual Size*

To Finish the Ribbon-wrapped Wreath:

1. Bend the metal ring into an oval shape.

2. Position the flower petal/frosted leaf spray near the top of the oval and wire it onto the metal ring. Position both amethyst rock sprays just to the right of the flower petal/frosted leaf spray and wire them onto the metal ring. Arrange the eleven frosted leaf sprays evenly around the perimeter of the oval and wire them onto the metal ring.

3. Cut the 26-gauge wire with wire cutters into one 6" length to make a hanger for the wreath. Slide three light pink seed and one crystal beads onto the length of wire. Repeat this sequence of beads for a total of eight combinations. Wire the hanger onto the metal ring at the top of the oval.

4. Beginning under the flower petals, wrap the metal ring with silk ribbon, making certain to cover all the twisted wires.

*Y*our favorite colors. Your daughter's favorite hairpin. That bottle that called to you at the flea market. Adding beadwork that is subtle or spectacular, delicate or bright, will add color, texture, and personality to every little corner of your world.

DECORATIVE BOTTLES

Antique Medicine Bottle with Open Heart

Photo on page 52.

Antique Medicine Bottle, 5" tall

Seed Beads, 11/0:
Crystal Lilac, Frosted Aquamarine, Frosted Blue Lilac, Frosted Pale Blue, Light Blue, Light Green, Lilac Ice, Sapphire Blue, 1 container each

11 Round Beads, 4mm: Blue Lace Agate

8 Round Beads, 6mm: Amazonite

24-gauge Wire: Silver

32-gauge Wire: Silver

Silk Ribbon, 7mm: Light Blue, $\frac{1}{2}$ yard

Wire Cutters

Needle-nosed Pliers

Instructions

1.   Cut the 24-gauge wire with wire cutters into one 18" length.

2.   Alternating colors, slide five light green and five frosted aquamarine seed beads onto the wire. Move the beads to the center of the wire. Bend the wire to form a loop and twist the wires just above the beads. Bend the remaining wire into a small heart shape.

3.   Working with one side of the extended wire, slide light green seed beads, blue lace agate round beads, and amazonite round beads onto the wire in the following order: seed, 4mm, seed, 6mm, seed, 4mm, seed, 6mm, seed, 4mm, seed, 6mm, seed, 4mm, seed, 6mm, seed, 4mm, seed, 6mm, seed, 4mm, 15 seed. Bend the wire back on itself so the beads do not slip off. Repeat with the remaining side of the extended wire.

4.   At the end of the seed beads on each wire, twist the wires together to secure the beads and bend the beaded wire into a small heart shape. See the illustration below.

5. Alternating colors, slide eight light green and eight frosted aquamarine seed beads onto one side of the remaining wire. Bend the wire to form a loop and twist the end of the wire to the center of the heart. Repeat with the remaining side of the wire. Trim the wires with wire cutters and flatten with needle-nosed pliers. See the illustration below.

6. Cut the 32-gauge wire into one 40" length.

7. Secure one end of the wire onto the top left side of the heart, five seed beads in from the 4mm bead.

8. Refer to the General Instructions for Making Twist Sprays on page 11. Use a combination of lilac and blue seed beads for each twist spray (14 sprays are needed). Slide 15 lilac and 15 blue seed beads onto the wire.

Bend the wire to form a loop, then twist the wire around itself and onto the top of the heart to secure. Twist the loop and tightly drape the wire approximately two seed beads away from the end of the first twist spray. Repeat with two different colors of lilac and blue seed beads for each twist spray.

9. Thread the ribbon through the seed bead loops at the top of the heart and tie the heart around the neck of an antique bottle.

Try hanging this beaded open heart from the key to an antique china cabinet or from the knob or handle of any vintage chest of drawers.

*F*rosted Medicine Bottle with Shamrocks & Butterflies

Frosted Antique Medicine Bottle, 5" tall

Specialty Beads, $\frac{1}{4}$"–$\frac{3}{8}$":
    6 Matte Emerald Shamrocks
    3 Matte Light Sapphire Butterflies
    3 Matte Sapphire Petite Flowers

Seed Beads, tiny holeless:
    Apple Green, Clear, 1 bag each

Industrial-strength Adhesive

Tacky Craft Glue & Glue Brush

Mixing Trays

Découpage Medium & Foam Brush

Instructions

1. Wipe the antique bottle and let dry.

2. Adhere the shamrock, butterfly, and petite flower beads randomly around the bottle with industrial-strength adhesive and let dry.

3. Working from the bottom up, daub tacky craft glue around $\frac{3}{4}$ of the bottle. Smooth the glue with a glue brush, making certain to avoid getting glue on the beads. Let the glue dry about one minute.

4. Hold the bottle over a mixing tray and pour the tiny holeless clear seed beads onto the bottle. Gently press the beads onto the glue and let dry.

5. Apply a very light coat of tacky craft glue over the clear beads on the bottle with a glue brush. Let the glue dry about one minute.

6. Hold the bottle over another mixing tray and pour the tiny holeless apple green seed beads over the entire beaded area. Gently press the beads onto the glue so there is minimal coverage of the apple green seed beads over the clear seed beads. Let dry.

7. Apply one coat of découpage medium with a foam brush over the entire beaded surface. Let dry.

utterfly-embellished Bottle

Frosted Bottle: Sunflower
Yellow, 12" tall

Seed Beads, 8/0:
Green Kaledioscope,
Wedgewood Blue,
1 container each

Seed Beads, 11/0:
Blue Lagoon, Cascade Green,
Sapphire Blue, 1 container each

2 Flat Beads, 6mm: Cobalt Blue

1 Round Bead, 8mm: Jade

1 Twisted Bead, 12mm x 8mm:
Turquoise Blue

24-gauge Wire: Silver

32-gauge Wire: Silver

Florist Tape

Silk Ribbon, 4mm: Blue, 1 yard

Wire Cutters

Needle-nosed Pliers

Straight Pin

Instructions

To Form the Upper Wings:

1. Cut the 24-gauge wire with wire cutters into two 30" lengths.

2. Slide 40 green kaledioscope seed beads onto one of the lengths of wire. Move the beads to the center of the wire and bend the wire to form a loop. Twist the wires together and bend the loop into a butterfly wing shape. Tighten the twists with needle-nosed pliers.

3. Repeat Step 2 for the remaining upper wing, but do not twist the two wings together. The upper wings must be "filled" before they are joined.

To Fill the Upper Wings:

1. Cut the 32-gauge wire into two 15" lengths.

2. Working with one wing at a time, tie one end of one of the lengths of wire to the most narrow part of the wing. Tightly drape the wire along the back side of the wing so it is between the first and second seed beads along the lower edge of the wing. Wrap the wire between the beads once.

3. Row 1: Slide one sapphire blue seed bead onto the wire. Extend the wire to the top edge of the wing and wrap it around the anchor wire between the first and second seed beads once.

4. Working from the top wing edge, tightly drape the wire along the back side of the wing so it is between the second and third seed beads. Wrap the wire between the beads once.

5. Row 2: Slide three sapphire blue seed beads onto the wire. Extend the wire to the bottom edge of the wing and wrap it around the anchor wire between the second and third seed beads once.

6. Working from the bottom wing edge, tightly drape the wire along the back side of the wing so it is between the third and fourth seed beads. Wrap the wire between the beads once.

7. Row 3: Slide four sapphire blue seed beads onto the wire. Extend the wire to the top edge of the wing and wrap it around the anchor wire between the third and fourth seed beads once.

Butterfly
Shown Actual Size

This butterfly can be easily wired to a pin to make a nice piece of jewelry or to a hairpin to make a lovely accessory to any hairdo.

8. Continue filling the wing with sapphire blue seed beads in the same manner (16 rows are needed to fill the upper wing).

9. Wrap the 32-gauge wire in-between two anchor wire beads, then trim away the excess wire. Tuck the wire ends in between the beads with a straight pin.

10. Repeat Steps 2–9 for the other upper wing.

11. Twist the two upper wings together. Tighten the twists with needle-nosed pliers.

To Form the Lower Wings:

1. Working with the wires from the upper wings, bend two of the wires upward. They should extend to the left and right of each other. Bend the remaining two wires downward.

2. Working with the wire on the left, slide 31 wedgewood blue seed beads onto the wire. Bend the wire to form a loop and twist the loop to anchor the wing.

3. Repeat Step 2 for the wire on the right.

To Fill the Lower Wings:

1. Cut the 32-gauge wire into two 15" lengths.

2. Fill each wing with blue lagoon seed beads in the same manner the upper wings were filled (10 rows are needed to fill each lower wing).

3. Twist the two lower wings together. Tighten the twists with needle-nosed pliers. Shape the upper and lower wings.

To Form the Body of the Butterfly:

1. Bend the wires on the lower wings upward to the center back of the butterfly, then bend them downward over the center front of the butterfly. At this time, do nothing with the wires from the upper wings.

2. Slide the jade round bead and the turquoise blue twisted bead onto both of the wires. Separate the wires and slide approximately

13 sapphire blue seed beads onto each wire. Bend the wires to the back of the twisted bead and upward toward the upper wings on the back side of the butterfly.

3.   Twist the wires together and then around the center of the butterfly to anchor the wires. Twist the wires together and bend them downward. Wrap the twisted wires with florist tape and silk ribbon for a finished look.

To Form the Antennae:

1.   Working with one of the wires on the upper wings, slide nine blue lagoon and nine cascade green seed beads onto the wire alternating the colors. Slide one cobalt blue flat bead and one cascade green seed bead onto the wire. Slide the beads down the wire to meet the round bead.

2.   Holding the beads snugly together, tightly coil the wire end several times with needle-nosed pliers. Flatten the coil against the uppermost seed bead, then trim away the excess wire with wire cutters.

3.   Repeat Steps 1 and 2 for the remaining wire. Attach the butterfly to the neck of the bottle.

HAIRPIN

Dragonfly Hairpin

Two-pronged hairpin:
Tortoiseshell, 4"-long

Seed Beads, 11/0:
Sea Blue, 1 container

Seed Beads, petite:
Crystal Aqua, 1 container

Round Crystal Beads, 4mm:
45 Sea Blue, 20 Sapphire Blue

Rondele Crystal Beads, 4mm:
20 Sea Blue, 13 Sapphire Blue

1 Round Crystal Bead, 6mm:
Olive Green

1 Glass Heart, 8mm: Frosted Blue

24-gauge Wire: Silver

32-gauge Wire: Silver

Silk Ribbon, 4mm: Brown, 1 yard

Wire Cutters

Needle-nosed Pliers

Straight Pin

Instructions

To Form the Upper Wings:

1.   Cut the 24-gauge wire with wire cutters into two 30" lengths.

2.   Slide 20 sea blue round crystal beads onto one of the lengths of wire. Move the beads to the center of the wire and bend the wire to form a loop. Twist the wires together and bend the loop into a dragonfly wing shape. Tighten the twists with needle-nosed pliers.

3.   Repeat Step 2 for the remaining upper wing, but do not twist the two wings together. The upper wings must be "filled" before they are joined.

To Fill the Upper Wings:

1.   Cut the 32-gauge wire into two 15" lengths.

2.   Working with one wing at a time, tie one end of one of the lengths of wire to the most narrow part of the wing. Tightly drape the wire along the back side of the wing so it is between the first and second round beads along the lower edge of the wing. Wrap the wire between the beads twice.

3.   Row 1: Slide one sea blue rondele crystal bead onto the wire. Extend the wire to the top edge of the wing and wrap it around the anchor wire between the first and second round beads twice.

4.   Working from the top wing edge, tightly drape the wire along the back side of the wing so it is between the second and third round beads. Wrap the wire between the beads twice.

5.   Row 2: Slide one sea blue seed, one sea blue rondele crystal, and one sea blue seed beads onto the wire. Extend the wire to the bottom edge of the wing and wrap it around the anchor wire between the second and third round beads twice.

6.   Continue filling the wing with sea blue and sapphire blue rondele crystal and sea blue seed beads in the same manner (8 rows are needed to fill the upper wing).

7.   Wrap the 32-gauge wire in between two anchor wire beads, then trim away the excess wire. Tuck the wire ends in between the beads with a straight pin.

8.   Repeat Steps 2–7 for the other upper wing.

9.   Twist the two upper wings together. Tighten the twists with needle-nosed pliers.

To Form the Lower Wings:

1.   Working with the wires from the upper wings, bend two of the wires upward. They should extend to the left and right of each other. Bend the remaining two wires downward.

2.   Working with the wire on the left, slide three sea blue seed, five sapphire blue round crystal, three sea blue seed, five sapphire blue round crystal, and three sea blue seed beads onto the wire. Bend the wire to form a loop and twist the loop to anchor the wing.

3.   Repeat Step 2 for the wire on the right.

4.   Twist the two lower wings together. Tighten the twists with needle-nosed pliers. Shape the upper and lower wings.

5.   Bend one wire to the left and one wire downward.

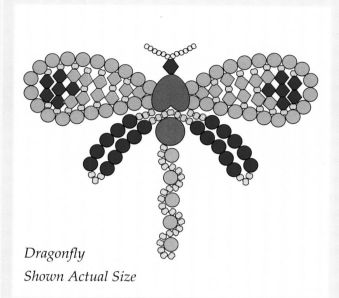

Dragonfly
Shown Actual Size

To Form the Tail of the Dragonfly:

1.   Slide five sea blue round crystal beads onto the wire facing downward. Move the beads to the center of the wire.

2.   Slide five sea blue seed beads onto the free wire. Bend the wire around the first round bead in the chain and wrap it around the wire with the beads, just below the first bead, to anchor it. Pull the wires taut. The seed beads will encircle half of the bead. Repeat with another five seed beads, this time encircling the next bead on the opposite side, creating an "S" curve or serpentine around the beads.

3.   Continue to serpentine the seed beads around the round beads. Twist the wires together below the last bead.

To Form the Body of the Dragonfly:

1.   Slide the olive green round crystal bead onto the "tail" wire. Bring the wire from the left (*To Form the Lower Wings,* Step 5) upward to meet the tail wire. Slide one sea blue seed bead, the frosted blue glass heart, one sapphire blue rondele crystal, and approximately eight sea blue seed beads onto both of the wires. Bend the wires to the back side of the dragonfly (the seed beads will not show).

To Form the Antennae:

1.   Cut the 32-gauge wire into one 12" length.

2.   At the center of the wire, invisibly tie the wire to the body of the dragonfly just below the frosted blue glass heart. Slide both of the wires through the heart bead. Separate the wires and slide six crystal aqua petite seed beads onto the wire on the left. Bend the wire around the last petite seed bead and back through the remaining five seed beads. Slide the wire through the rondele bead again, pulling it taut so the petite seed beads fit snugly against the rondele crystal bead.

3.   Repeat Step 2 for the remaining wire.

4.   Bend the 32-gauge wire to the back side of the dragonfly. Twist the wires together and trim.

5.   Bend the 24-gauge wire downward and attach the dragonfly to the hairpin. Wrap the twisted wires with silk ribbon for a finished look.

DECORATIVE BOX

Sheer sticky tape is sold in sheets and on a roll, but either type has a protective covering. Once this covering has been removed, avoid touching the adhesive so the strength of the tape is not compromised.

Flower Garden Trinket Box

Wooden Box, 4" x 2" x 3" high

Acrylic Paints: Blue, Green, White

Paintbrush

Seed Beads, 11/0:
   Crystal Multi-Blue, 1 container

Seed Beads, petite:
   Crystal Aqua, 1 container

Seed Beads, tiny holeless:
   Apple Green, Clear, Silver,
   Teal, 1 bag each

Premixed Seed/Bugle Beads:
   Leaf Green, Pearl, 1-oz. jar each

Specialty Beads, assorted small:
   2 Matte Red Tulip
   9 Matte Light Pink Flowers
   3 Matte Ruby Hearts
   1 Clear Crystal Butterfly
   9 Assorted Green Leaves

Sheer Sticky Tape, 9" x 11" sheet

Scissors

Mixing Trays

Découpage Medium & Foam Brush

Needle-nosed Pliers

Instructions

1. Paint the bottom of the wooden box and the bottom third of all sides with one coat of green paint and let dry. Paint the middle third of all sides with one coat of blue paint and let dry. Paint the top third of all sides and the top of the box with one coat of white paint and let dry.

2. Cut the sheer sticky tape with scissors to cover the front side of the box and lid (the tape should be separated where the box and lid meet). Add an extra $\frac{1}{4}$" to the width of the box to allow the tape to overlap on each side. Align the tape along the bottom edge of the box and adhere in place. Remove the plastic covering from the tape, but do not discard.

3. Beginning $\frac{1}{4}$" from the bottom of the box, randomly position green bugle beads for stems and a variety of specialty beads for flowers and leaves with needle-nosed pliers to avoid touching the tape with your fingers. Add the butterfly to the front of the box.

4. Cover the front of the box with the plastic covering, exposing only the bottom $\frac{1}{4}$". Hold the box over a mixing tray and pour the leaf green premixed seed/bugle beads onto the exposed tape at the bottom of the box. Gently press the beads onto the tape.

5. Cover the front of the box with the plastic covering, exposing only the bottom third. Hold the box over another mixing tray and pour the apple green tiny holeless seed beads onto the exposed tape to create the landscape. Gently press the beads onto the tape.

6. Repeat Step 5, exposing only the middle third of the box. Use teal tiny holeless seed, crystal multi-blue 11/0 seed, and crystal aqua petite seed beads to create the sky.

7. Repeat Step 5, exposing only the top third of the box (the lid). Use teal and silver tiny holeless seed and pearl premixed seed/bugle beads to create more sky with clouds.

8. Repeat Steps 2–7 for the remaining sides of the box. Repeat Step 2 for the top of the box. Use clear tiny holeless seed and pearl premixed seed/bugle beads.

9. Apply two coats of découpage medium with a foam brush over the entire beaded surface to seal. Let dry between each coat.

WREATH

Crystal Leaf Wreath

Seed Beads, 11/0:
  Silver-lined Crystal,
  approximately 21,000

26-gauge Wire: Tinned Copper

Wire Cutters

Silver Metal Ring, 9"-diameter

This wreath has a total of 75 beaded leaves. Each leaf is made with 280 beads, making the total number of beads needed 21,000. A four-dram vial of beads contains 2,240 beads. You can purchase ten of these vials to give you enough beads or you can purchase a $\frac{1}{2}$ kilo of beads. A $\frac{1}{2}$ kilo contains approximately 56,000 beads.

Instructions

1.   Cut the wire with wire cutters into one 30" length for each leaf (75 leaves are needed).

2.   Refer to the General Instructions for Forming a Leaf or Flower Petal with a Basic Axis on pages 10–11. Begin the axis with ten beads for the center and form five rows of beads around the axis. Cut the knot from the tip of the axis. Fold the top axis wire down toward the back of the leaf. Wrap the wire snugly around the bottom of the axis twice.

3.   Wire the leaves together in sets of three (25 sets are needed).

4.   Wire the sets of leaves onto the metal ring and make a hanger from wire.

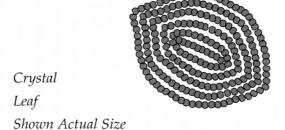

Crystal
Leaf
Shown Actual Size

BOBBY PINS

Bug Bobby Pins

Bobby Pins, standard length

An Assortment of Beads:
   Any Size and Color or
   Combination of Sizes
   and Colors

32-gauge Wire: Silver

Wire Cutters

Needle-nosed Pliers

Each bug will need beads for the head, the neck, the body, the wings, and the antennae. Variations from this basic design are endless.

*Small Bugs
Shown Actual Size*

Bug

Shown Actual Size

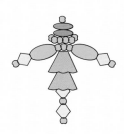

Bug

Shown Actual Size

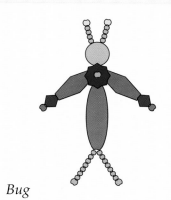

Bug

Shown Actual Size

Instructions

To Make One Small Bug:

1.   Cut the 32-gauge wire with wire cutters into one 20" length.

2.   Slide one teardrop-shaped and 15 petite seed beads onto the length of wire. Move the beads to the center of the wire and bend the wire to form a loop (one wing). Thread the wire back through the teardrop-shaped bead (the body) and tighten the wire. Slide 15 petite seed beads onto the wire on the opposite side. Bend the wire to form a loop (the other wing). Thread the wire back through the teardrop-shaped bead and tighten the wire.

3.   Wires will extend from both sides of the teardrop-shaped bead (body). Bend the wires to the sides and position the body and wings vertically over the bobby pin. Thread one wire end through and around the top of the bobby pin several times, pulling the wire tightly each time. Repeat with the wire on the opposite side. Make certain the beads are secure on the bobby pin, then extend the wires upward.

4.   Slide one round bead (the head) onto both wires. Push the bead as close to the top of the teardrop-shaped bead as possible (there will be a slight gap between the beads).

5.   Separate the wires at the top of the round bead. Slide two to four petite seed and one 11/0 seed beads (the antennae) onto one of the wire ends. Thread the wire back through the petite seed and round beads and tighten the wire so the petite seed beads rest against the round bead. Repeat for the remaining antennae.

6.   Wires will extend from the bottom of the round bead (head). Slide several seed beads onto both of the wires. Wrap these beads around the "neck" of the bug, between the head and the body, to cover the gap. Secure the wires around the bobby pin. Trim the wires with wire cutters and flatten with needle-nosed pliers.

SENTIMENT

Using different shades of seed beads for each letter helps the eye see the letter more easily. The seed beads are used to cover a lot of territory and help add definition to the specialty beads.

Dream Script

Seed Beads, 11/0:

Multi-Peach, Multi-Pink, 1 container each

Round Beads, 4mm:

24 Rhodonite, 28 Rose Quartz

10 Round Crystal Beads, 4mm: Light Rose

12 Rondele Crystal Beads, 4mm: Light Rose

13 Cube-shaped Beads, 4mm x 6mm: Pink

5 Glass Hearts, 6mm: Frosted Pink

24-gauge Wire: Silver

Wire Cutters

Needle-nosed Pliers

Instructions

1.   Cut the 24-gauge wire with wire cutters into one 72" length.

2.   Bead and bend the wire into the word "Dream", one letter at a time, in the same manner as the word would be written in cursive writing.

3.   Randomly slide the beads onto the length of wire as desired. Twist the wire or wrap it around itself with needle-nosed pliers as necessary to hold the letters in place.

4.   To finish, wrap the wire ends onto the beaded wire and trim.

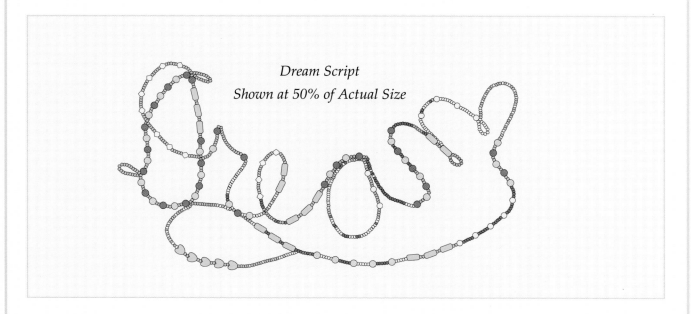

Dream Script
Shown at 50% of Actual Size

EVERYDAY ADORNMENTS

When is a bottle more than a container? How can you frame beautiful flowers on your wall? When does a bug become a treasured keepsake? Bright beadwork, ribbons, and a little magic can transform everyday objects into enchanting touches of artistry.

GARLAND

Garland-wrapped Bottle

Frosted Bottle: Coral, 12" tall

Seed Beads, 11/0:
    Christmas Green, Light Green,
    Opaline Tea Rose, 1 container each

9 Pearls, 4mm: Peach

26-gauge Wire: Lavender

Wire Cutters

Needle-nosed Pliers

Instructions

1. Cut the 26-gauge wire with wire cutters into one 70" length (the finished garland will be approximately 17" long).

2. Bend the wire in half lengthwise and form a loop at the closed end. Beginning $\frac{1}{4}$" from the loop, twist the two wires together for a length of 2".

3. Separate the wires and bend the wire on the left upward, leaving the remaining wire straight. Slide 12 Christmas green seed beads onto the left wire, making certain the beads fit snugly against the straight wire.

4. Bend the beaded wire to form a small loop and wrap the looped wire taut around itself at the base of the loop to make a "leaf." Twist the two wires together for a length of $\frac{1}{2}$".

5. Separate the wires and bend the wire on the right upward, leaving the remaining wire straight. Slide 12 light green seed beads onto the right wire, making certain the beads fit snugly against the straight wire. Repeat Step 4.

6. Separate the wires and slide one peach pearl onto one of the wires, making certain the pearl fits snugly against the twists in the wires. Keep this wire straight. Slide five or six opaline tea rose seed beads onto the remaining wire, making certain the beads fit snugly against the twists in the wires next to the pearl. Bend the beaded wire so it encircles half of the pearl, then wrap it around the straight wire at the upper end of the pearl. Slide five or six more opaline tea rose seed beads onto the same wire, making certain the beads fit snugly against the previous seed beads on that wire. Bend the beaded wire so it encircles the remaining half of the pearl, then wrap it around the straight wire at the twists in the wires to make a "flower." See the illustrations at the top of the next column.

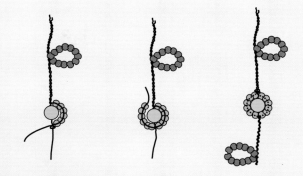

7. Bend the wire so it lays underneath the pearl and becomes parallel with the straight wire containing the pearl. Twist the two wires together for a length of $\frac{1}{2}$" to repeat this sequence of looped leaves and flowers (9 flowers are needed).

8. When the beaded garland is complete, twist the two wires together and trim with wire cutters.

9. Wrap the garland around the bottle as desired.

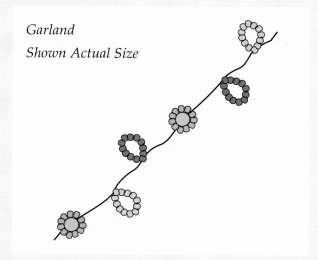

Garland
Shown Actual Size

FRUIT

Strawberries & Limes

5 Plastic Strawberries
 with Stems

2 Plastic Limes with Stems

Seed Beads, 11/0:
 Black, Yellow,
 1 container each

Premixed Seed/Bugle Beads:
 Leaf Green, Raspberry,
 1-oz. jar each

Seed Beads, tiny holeless:
 Apple Green, Gold, Red,
 1 bag each

15 Velvet Leaves, 1" x 1 $\frac{1}{2}$":
 Hunter Green

26-gauge Wire: Silver

Florist Tape

Mixing Trays

Tacky Craft Glue & Glue Brush

Découpage Medium & Foam Brush

Scissors

Pinking Shears

Wire Cutters

Instructions

To Bead the Strawberries:

1.   Remove the calyxes from the plastic strawberries if applicable, but leave the stems attached.

2.   Working with one at a time, daub tacky craft glue around each strawberry. Smooth the glue with a glue brush. Let the glue dry about one minute.

3. Pour a small amount of black seed beads and the jar of raspberry premixed seed/bugle beads into a mixing tray to combine.

4. Hold each strawberry over another mixing tray and pour the bead mixture onto the strawberries. Gently press the beads onto the glue.

5. Hold the strawberries over another mixing tray and pour the red tiny holeless seed beads over the entire beaded area. Gently press the beads onto the glue. Repeat and let dry.

6. Apply one coat of découpage medium with a foam brush over the entire beaded surface to seal. Let dry.

7. Wrap florist tape around each stem.

8. Cut one five-pointed calyx from the velvet leaves for each strawberry. Cut a small slit to the center and slide one around each stem. Glue in place with tacky craft glue.

To Bead the Limes:

1. Working with one at a time, daub tacky craft glue around each lime. Smooth the glue with a glue brush. Let the glue dry about one minute.

2. Hold each lime over a mixing tray and pour yellow seed beads onto the upper half of the limes. Gently press the beads onto the glue.

3. Hold the limes over another mixing tray and pour the gold tiny holeless seed beads over the yellow seed beads. Gently press the beads onto the glue.

4. Hold the limes over another mixing tray and pour the leaf green premixed seed/bugle beads over the bottom half of the limes. Gently press the beads onto the glue.

5. Hold the limes over another mixing tray and pour the apple green tiny holeless seed beads over the leaf green bead mixture and a small amount onto the yellow seed beads. Gently press the beads onto the glue and let dry.

6. Apply one coat of découpage medium with a foam brush over the entire beaded surface to seal. Let dry.

7. Glue the top edge of one velvet leaf onto the bottom edge of another velvet leaf, overlapping the leaves about $\frac{1}{2}$". Repeat until you have five velvet leaves made from ten velvet leaves.

8. Trim the leaves into long, narrow leaves with pinking shears.

9. Cut the 26-gauge wire with wire cutters into one 6" length. Wire the lime stems together and straighten the remaining wire. Wire the leaves onto the straightened wire.

10. Wrap the twisted wires with florist tape for a finished look.

PANSY BOUQUETS

Using the instructions given to make pansy petals on pages 40–41, proceed making three complete pansies with metallic multi-plum seed beads. Make the centers with marigold seed beads and the leaves with olive green seed beads. Wrap the twisted wire stems with embroidery floss for a finished look and tie a piece of ribbon into a bow around the bouquet.

Metallic Plum-colored Pansy Bouquet

Seed Beads, 11/0:
    Marigold, Metallic Multi-Plum,
    Olive Green, 1 container each

26-gauge Wire: Silver

Mesh Ribbon, 1"-wide:
    Olive Green, $\frac{3}{4}$ yard

Embroidery Floss: Olive Green

Wire Cutters

Needle-nosed Pliers

Plum-colored, Crystal-edged Pansy Bouquet

Seed Beads, 11/0:
    Ice, Marigold, Metallic Plum,
    Olive Green, 1 container each

26-gauge Wire: Silver

Ribbon, $1\frac{1}{2}$"-wide:
    Silver/Mauve, $\frac{3}{4}$ yard

Embroidery Floss: Olive Green

Wire Cutters

Needle-nosed Pliers

Using the instructions given to make pansy petals on pages 40–41, proceed making three complete pansies with metallic plum and ice seed beads. Make the centers with marigold seed beads and the leaves with olive green seed beads. Make three pansy buds with ice seed beads. Wrap the twisted wire stems with embroidery floss for a finished look and tie a piece of ribbon into a bow around the bouquet.

ROSES

Red Rose Pin

Seed Beads, 11/0:

    Antique Red, Bay Leaf
    Green, Emerald Green,
    Multi-Red, 1 container each

Seed Beads, petite:

    Black, Red, 1 container each

5 Bugle Beads, small: Antique Red

1 Pearl, 4mm

1 Round Crystal Bead, 4mm: Red

1 Teardrop-shaped Crystal Bead,
    4mm x 8mm: Red

26-gauge Wire: Green

32-gauge Wire: Silver

Silk Ribbon, 7mm:

    Olive Green, $\frac{1}{2}$ yard

Pin Back, 1": Silver

Wire Cutters

Needle-nosed Pliers

Instructions

To Make the Rose Petals:

1. Cut the 26-gauge wire with wire cutters into five 30" lengths. Tie a knot at one end of each length of wire.

2. Refer to the General Instructions for Forming a Leaf or Flower Petal with a Basic Axis on pages 10–11. Slide one bugle and one antique red seed bead onto one of the lengths of wire, positioning the bead 2" below the knot. Proceed with forming the center axis.

3. Alternating shades of red, form five rows of seed beads and wrap them around the center axis.

All Shown Actual Size

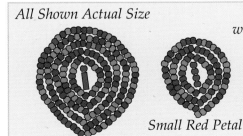

Large Red Petal

Small Red Petal

*Small Red Petal
with Additional Row of
Red Seed Beads*

*Beaded Loop
(Center)*

Leaf

*Bumblebee on
Beaded Tether*

4. Repeat Steps 2 and 3 to make four more large red petals (5 petals are needed).

5. Cut the 26-gauge wire into three 20" lengths. Tie a knot at one end of each length of wire.

6. Slide four antique red seed beads onto one of the lengths of wire, positioning the beads 2" below the knot. Proceed with forming the center axis.

7. Alternating shades of red, form three rows of seed beads and wrap them around the center axis.

8. Repeat Steps 6 and 7 to make two more small red petals, forming one additional row of red seed beads so these two petals are one row larger than the previous small red petal (3 petals are needed).

9. Cut the 26-gauge wire into one 8" length. Tie a knot at one end of the length of wire.

10. Slide eight antique red seed beads, one 4mm pearl, and eight more antique red seed beads onto the wire. Move the beads to the center of the wire. Bend the wire to form a loop and twist the wire just above the beads. Make certain the pearl is at the top center.

11. Arrange the three small petals next to each other, evenly spaced, and twist the wires together. Arrange the five large petals around the three small joined petals and twist the wires together. Slip the beaded loop with the pearl at the top center through the center of the three small petals and twist the wires together. Tighten the twists with needle-nosed pliers.

To Make the Leaf:

1. Cut the 26-gauge wire with wire cutters into one 30" length. Tie a knot at one end of the length of wire.

2. Slide four emerald green seed beads onto the wire, positioning the beads 2" below the knot. Proceed with forming the center axis.

3. Alternating shades of green, form five rows of seed beads and wrap them around the center axis.

4. Arrange the leaf under one large petal and twist the wires together. Trim the wires to $2\frac{1}{2}$" long on the back side of the rose.

5. Wrap the twisted wires with silk ribbon for a finished look. Position the pin back on the rose stem and secure it with silk ribbon.

To Make the Bumblebee:

1. Using the instructions given to make Bug Bobby Pins on pages 68–69, proceed making the bumblebee with round crystal, teardrop-shaped crystal, and black and red petite seed beads.

2. Make a beaded tether with black and red petite seed beads and wire the tether onto one large petal so the bumblebee is flying about 1" above the petal.

Red Rose and Bumblebee Shown Actual Size

pening
Rose Bud

Seed Beads, 11/0:
Aspen Green, Ballet Pink,
Coral, Emerald Green,
Light Pink, Mint Green,
Olive Green, Pearl, Pink
Lemonade, 1 container each

Seed Beads, tiny holeless:
Clear, 1 bag

26-gauge Wire: Green

26-gauge Wire: Silver

9 Velvet Leaves, 1" x 1 $\frac{1}{2}$":
Hunter Green

Silk Ribbon, 7mm:
Olive Green, $\frac{1}{2}$ yard

Sheer Ribbon, 1"-wide:
Light Pink, $\frac{3}{4}$ yard

Mixing Tray

Tacky Craft Glue
& Glue Brush

Découpage Medium
& Foam Brush

Knitting Needle

Wire Cutters

Needle-nosed Pliers

*Using the instructions given to make rose petals on pages 80–81,
proceed making eight rose petals the same size with ballet pink, coral,
light pink, pearl, and pink lemonade seed beads on silver 26-gauge
wire. Use a knitting needle to mold the center petal vertically so it
wraps around itself and looks like a petal just beginning to open.
Make three different sized leaves with aspen green, emerald green,
mint green, and olive green seed beads on green 26-gauge wire. Using
the instructions given to make frosted velvet leaves on page 23, glue
the clear tiny holeless seed beads onto three of the nine velvet leaves.
Wire the frosted velvet leaves to the rose and leaves. Wrap the twisted
wire stems with silk ribbon for a finished look and tie a piece of sheer
ribbon into a bow around the single rose stem.*

ORNAMENT

Hanging Heart Ornament

Velvet-covered Heart Ornament

Seed Beads, 11/0:
   Coral, Cream, Forest Green,
   Fuchsia, Green Ice, Mauve,
   Peach Ice, Pearl, Pink Ice,
   Raspberry, 1 container each

1 Specialty Bead, assorted small:
   Matte Pink Flower

26-gauge Wire: Green

32-gauge Wire: Bare Copper

Embroidery Floss:
   Olive Green, Sage Green

Mixing Trays

Tacky Craft Glue & Glue Brush

Wire Cutters

Needle-nosed Pliers

Twist the sage green embroidery floss and tie a knot at one end. Adhere the twisted embroidery floss to the top of the velvet-covered heart ornament with the tacky craft glue, making certain to leave a loop at the top for hanging. Using the instructions given for the Terra-cotta Mini Vase on pages 14–15, proceed gluing the cream, peach ice, and pearl seed beads on top of the velvet-covered heart ornament over the twisted floss. Randomly glue some raspberry seed beads around the outer edge of the heart. Refer to the General Instructions for Forming a Leaf or Flower Petal with a Basic Axis on pages 10–11. Make small flower petals using coral, fuchsia, mauve, and pink ice seed beads. Repeat, using forest green and green ice seed beads for the leaves. Use the small pink flower specialty bead for the center of the flower and wrap the twisted stems with olive green embroidery floss for a finished look. Arrange to fit on top of the beaded heart ornament and adhere in place with tacky craft glue.

PAPERWEIGHT

Heirloom Paperweight

Clear Glass Paperweight, $3\frac{1}{2}$"-diameter

Seed Beads, 11/0: Jade, 1 container

Seed Beads, tiny holeless:
Brown, Red, 1 bag each

1 Antique Button, 1"

7 Rose Cabachons, 10mm: Coral

5 Specialty Beads, $\frac{1}{4}$": Crystal Leaves

Velvet Leaves, 1" x $1\frac{1}{2}$":
1 Beige/Green; 8 Burgundy/Green

Lace Scraps: Light Pink

Silk Ribbon, 4mm: Heather, 6"

Silver/Rhinestone Piece of Jewelry

Tissue Paper: Metallic Gold, 4" square

Sheer Sticky Tape, 9" x 11" sheet

Tacky Craft Glue

Scissors

Mixing Trays

Wire Cutters

Needle-nosed Pliers

Instructions

1.   Cut the tissue paper with scissors to fit over the bottom of the backing piece on the paperweight and adhere in place to create the background color.

2.   Cut the sheer sticky tape with scissors to fit over the tissue paper and adhere in place. Remove the plastic covering from the tape and trim the tape around the edges of the backing piece on the paperweight.

3.   Remove the shaft from the back of the antique button with wire cutters as closely as possible. Position the button on the center of the backing piece with needle-nosed pliers to avoid touching the tape with your fingers. Add the rose cabochons around the button and position the crystal leaf beads along the right edge. Cut one of the beige/green velvet leaves in half with scissors and position them

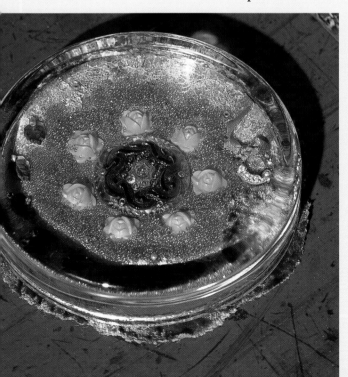

near the top. Position the scraps of lace along the left edge. Tie a tiny silk ribbon bow around the piece of silver/rhinestone jewelry and position it near the end of one of the velvet leaf halves. Drape the excess ribbon over the edge and gently press the items onto the tape.

4.   Hold the backing piece over a mixing tray and pour the brown tiny holeless seed beads onto the exposed tape. Gently press the beads onto the tape.

5.   Hold the backing piece over another mixing tray and pour the red tiny holeless seed beads over the brown ones. Gently press the beads onto the tape.

6.   Individually adhere one jade seed bead on top of each crystal leaf bead with tacky craft glue and randomly scatter a few on top of the beaded design.

7.   Trim the beaded backing piece all around. Position the beaded design right side up into the paperweight. While holding the design firmly in place, draw a bead of tacky craft glue around the outer edges between the backing piece and the paperweight and adhere together.

8.   Adhere seven burgundy/green velvet leaves around the bottom of the paperweight with tacky craft glue, extending the leaves about $\frac{1}{8}$" from the outer edge. Adhere the remaining velvet leaf to the bottom center of the paperweight.

HOLIDAY DECOR

Holly Leaf & Berry Napkin Ring

Seed Beads, 11/0:
   Aspen Green, Mint Green,
   1 container each

5 Round Beads, 6mm: Ruby Red

26-gauge Wire: Bare Copper

32-gauge Wire: Bare Copper

Metal Ring, 1 $\frac{1}{2}$"-diameter

Wire Cutters

Needle-nosed Pliers

Instructions

To Make One Napkin Ring:

1.   Cut the 26-gauge wire with wire cutters into one 30" length. Tie one end of the length of wire onto the metal ring.

2.   Slide one mint green seed, one aspen green seed, and one mint green seed beads onto the length of wire. Move the beads snugly against the ring. Wrap the wire around the ring so the beads rest on the outer side. Continue to slide seed beads onto the wire in the same sequence and wrap the wire around the ring until the ring is covered with beads. Secure the wire and trim with wire cutters.

3.   Cut the 26-gauge wire into one 10" length.

4.   Slide 100 mint green seed beads onto the length of wire. Bend the wire to form a loop and twist the wires together below the bottom beads. Bend the wire loop into a holly leaf shape.

5.   Cut the 32-gauge wire into one 30" length.

6.   Tie the length of wire onto the holly leaf at the base. Slide aspen green seed beads onto the length of wire for an area of approximately 2". Extend the wire to the opposite end of the leaf, making certain there are enough seed beads on the wire to cover the complete extension. Wrap the wire around the upper tip of the leaf to anchor in place.

7.   Drape the wire along the back of the holly leaf to the outside edge, three beads to the left of center. Wrap the wire between the third and fourth seed beads once.

8.   Slide one mint green seed bead onto the wire. Extend the wire across the leaf and wrap it around the center row in between the beads. Slide one more mint green seed bead onto the wire. Extend the wire across the leaf

to the opposite edge and wrap it between the third and fourth seed beads once.

9. Drape the wire along the back of the holly leaf to the outside edge. Wrap the wire in between the fourth and fifth seed beads once. Repeat Step 9, adding enough seed beads to fill the wire, then wrapping the wire in between the fourth and fifth seed beads.

10. Continue to fill the holly leaf in the same manner, using the aspen green seed beads to shade the center of the holly leaf.

11. Repeat Steps 4–11 to make two more holly leaves (3 holly leaves are needed).

12. Arrange the holly leaves and twist the wires together. Wire the leaves onto the beaded ring. Trim the wires and flatten with needle-nosed pliers.

13. Cut the 26-gauge wire with wire cutters into one 10" length.

14. Slide one round bead onto the length of wire. Move the bead to the center of the wire and twist the wire around the bottom of the bead. Separate the wires and slide one round bead onto one of the wires. Twist the wire around the bottom of the bead. Slide one round bead onto the other wire. Twist the wire around the bottom of the bead. Continue until all five round beads have been added to the wire. Slip the round bead cluster (berries) through the center of the three holly leaves and twist the wires to the ring. Tighten the twists with needle-nosed pliers.

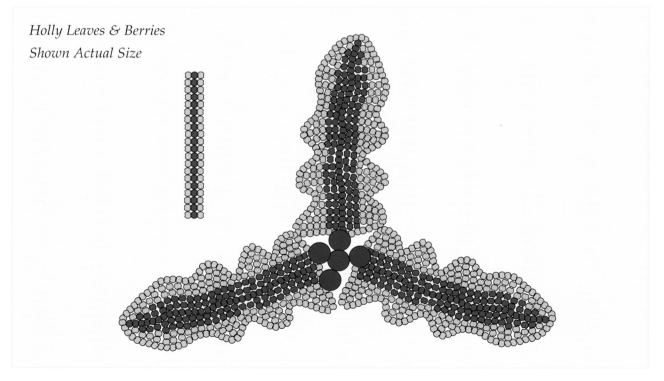

Holly Leaves & Berries
Shown Actual Size

Using the instructions given to make a small bug on page 69, proceed making the flying insect. Use the beads specified for the head, the neck, the body, the large and small wings, and the antennae. Make a beaded tether with a combination of bugle and seed beads to the desired length and wire the tether onto the back of the flying insect.

INQUISITIVE INSECT

Red & Black Insect

Seed Beads, 11/0:
    Black, Red, 1 container each

Seed Beads, petite:
    Black, 1 container

Bugle Beads, small:
    Black, 1 container

1 Round Bead, 6mm: Red

3 Round Crystal Beads, 4mm: Red

1 Teardrop-shaped Bead,
    20mm x 8mm: Black

2 Teardrop-shaped Beads,
    8mm x 4mm: Black

32-gauge Wire: Silver

Wire Cutters

Needle-nosed Pliers

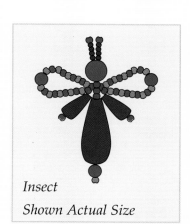

*Insect
Shown Actual Size*

FLOWERS & FLOURISHES

In your personal living spaces and daily life, it is the addition of small, unique touches that create personality and charm. From the intricate texture of a beaded flower to the subtle dimension of a beaded lamp shade, the interest is always in the details!

HYACINTH

Hyacinth in Bloom

Photo on page 90.

Seed Beads, 11/0:
  Amethyst, Metallic Plum, Orchid,
  Periwinkle, Spearmint Green,
  1 container each

14-gauge Wire: Bare Copper

24-gauge Wire: Gold

Wire Cutters

Needle-nosed Pliers

Instructions

1.   Cut the 24-gauge wire with wire cutters into twenty-four 36" lengths. Tie a knot at one end of each length of wire.

2.   Slide 40 metallic plum seed beads onto one of the lengths of wire. Leaving a 7" extension of wire below the first bead, bend the wire so the beads form a loop. Twist the wires together just below the loop. Bend the beaded loop into a soft heart shape. Bend the 7" length of wire downward to create an anchor stem. See the illustration at the top of the next column.

3.   Bend the long wire up and over the bottom center of the loop. Slide 40 metallic plum seed beads onto the wire. Bend the wire so the beads form a second loop. Twist the wires together just below the loop. Bend the beaded loop into a soft heart shape. See the illustration below.

4.   Bend the wire up and over the bottom center of the second loop. Repeat Step 3 to form a third and a fourth heart-shaped loop to complete four petals for the bottom layer. Twist the long wire to the anchor stem.

5. Bend the long wire upward through the center of the four heart-shaped petals and slide 40 seed beads onto the wire. Repeat Steps 3 and 4 to complete four petals for the middle layer. Randomly use the amethyst, metallic plum, orchid, and periwinkle seed beads. Twist the petal wires to the anchor stem.

6. Bend the long wire upward through the center of the four heart-shaped petals and slide 40 seed beads onto the wire. Repeat Steps 3 and 4 to complete four petals for the top layer. Randomly use the amethyst, orchid, and periwinkle seed beads. Twist the petal wires to the anchor stem to complete the first three-layered flower.

7. Repeat Steps 2–6 to make 23 more three-layered flowers (24 flowers are needed).

8. Twist all 24 flowers together forming the hyacinth shape.

9. Cut the 14-gauge wire into four 18" lengths. Bend a small loop at one end of one of the lengths of wire with needle-nosed pliers.

Place the wires together next to the long stem, making certain the wire with the loop is at the opposite end, facing downward. Secure the wires together to create a thick, sturdy stem.

10. Cut the 24-gauge wire into one 90" length. Attach the wire to the bottom of the hyacinth at one side of the stem.

11. Slide spearmint green seed beads onto the wire for a length of 3". Very tightly wrap the beaded wire around the stem, then slide additional seed beads onto the wire for a length of 3". Continue to wrap the beaded wire around the stem, adding more beads as needed to cover the stem. Wrap the wire through the loop at the bottom of the stem several times to secure.

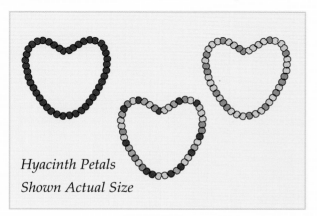

Hyacinth Petals
Shown Actual Size

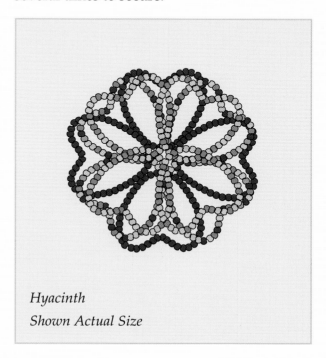

Hyacinth
Shown Actual Size

ORNAMENT

Topaz-tipped Star

Papier Mâché Star, 3"

Acrylic Paint: Metallic Gold

Paintbrush

Premixed Seed/Bugle Beads:
   Topaz, 1-oz. jar

Seed Beads, tiny holeless:
   Silver, 1 bag

6 Round Beads, 4mm: Gold

Straight Pins, $1\frac{1}{6}$"

Mixing Trays

Tacky Craft Glue & Glue Brush

Découpage Medium & Foam Brush

Instructions

1.   Paint the star (front and back) with one coat of metallic gold paint and let dry.

2.   Working with the front of the star, daub tacky craft glue in an uneven manner onto the center of the star, stopping approximately $\frac{3}{4}$" from each star point. Smooth the glue with a glue brush. Let the glue dry about one minute.

3.   Hold the star over a mixing tray and pour the tiny holeless seed beads onto the star. Gently press the beads onto the glue and let dry.

4.   Daub tacky craft glue onto each star point. Smooth the glue with a glue brush. Let the glue dry about one minute.

5.   Hold the star over another mixing tray and pour the premixed seed/bugle beads onto the star points. Gently press the beads onto the glue. Immediately pour the tiny holeless seed beads onto the star points. Gently press the beads onto the glue.

6.   Repeat Steps 4 and 5 for the back of the star.

7.   Apply one coat of découpage medium with a foam brush over the entire beaded surface to seal. Let dry.

8.   Slide one round bead onto a straight pin. Daub tacky craft glue onto the straight pin just below the bead. Push the straight pin into the star at a point. Repeat until each star point and the front center of the star has a bead.

LAMP

Lamp with Beaded Shade

Candlestick Lamp for Glass Votive or Bulb

Metal Lamp Shade,
    to fit over glass votive or bulb

Seed Beads, 6/0:
    Chartreuse, approximately 1400

16 Glass Drops, 10mm x 6mm: Peridot

26-gauge Wire: Tinned Copper

Jump Rings

Wire Cutters

Instructions

1. Cut the wire with wire cutters into one 72" length. Beginning at a "spoke" in the lamp shade, twist one wire end around the bottom edge of the lamp shade until it is secure. Wrap the wire around the bottom edge while forming a small loop that extends down from the bottom edge, spacing the loops about 1" apart. Continue around the bottom edge of the lamp shade. Secure the wire and trim with wire cutters.

2. Cut the wire with wire cutters into one 90" length. Beginning at a spoke in the lamp shade, twist one wire end around the top edge of the lamp shade until it is secure.

3. Slide chartreuse seed beads onto the wire until the beads on the wire will cover the space from the first spoke to the next. Extend the beaded wire to the second spoke and snugly wrap the wire around the spoke so the beads cover the top edge of the lamp shade.

4. Continue to slide seed beads onto the wire, extending the beaded wire to the next adjacent spoke and securing the wire in place each time. Cover the entire lamp shade with beaded wire, making certain the beaded rows fit snugly against each other. Attach additional lengths of wire as needed.

5. Attach the glass drops to the loops along the bottom edge of the lamp shade with jump rings.

Margarita Bouquet with Fern-style Leaves

Seed Beads, 11/0:
> Christmas Green, Green Ice, Light Green, 1 container each

Bugle Beads, small:
> Peppermint, 1 container

77 Round Beads, 3mm:
> Mother of Pearl

11 Round Beads, 4mm:
> Light Mauve Freshwater Pearl

26-gauge Wire: Flesh

32-gauge Wire: Silver

3 Velvet Leaves, 1" x 1½": Beige/Green

Florist Tape

Wire Cutters

Needle-nosed Pliers

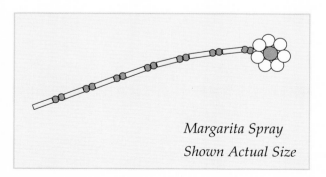

Margarita Spray
Shown Actual Size

Instructions

To Make the Margarita Sprays:

1.   Cut the 32-gauge wire with wire cutters into eleven 15" lengths.

2.   Slide seven 3mm round beads onto one of the lengths of wire to make the first spray. Move the beads to the center of the wire.

3.   Slide one wire end around and back through the seven round beads forming a circle. Pull the wire ends taut and twist the wires together. Bend the wires down toward the center of the circle.

4.   Slide one 4mm round bead onto both of the wires. Move the bead to the center of the circle. Wrap the wires around the opposite side of the circle once.

5.   Slide two light green seed and one peppermint bugle beads onto both of the wires. Repeat this sequence of beads for a total of seven combinations.

6.   Repeat Steps 2–5 to make ten more margarita sprays (11 sprays are needed).

To Make the Fern-style Leaves:

1. Cut the 26-gauge wire with wire cutters into three 15" lengths.

2. Alternating shades of green, slide three seed, one bugle, nine seed, one bugle, and three seed beads onto one of the lengths of wire. Move the beads to the center of the wire. Bend the wire in half to form a loop. Twist the wires together below the bottom beads.

3. Separate the wires and slide seven assorted green seed, one bugle, and 12 assorted green seed beads onto each wire. Bend the wires in half to form a loop on each side of the original loop. Twist the wires together and tighten the twists with needle-nosed pliers.

4. Extend the wires downward. Slide five assorted green seed, one bugle, and three assorted green seed beads onto each wire. Twist the wires together below the bottom beads.

5. Separate the wires and slide four assorted green seed, one bugle, and 19 assorted green seed beads onto each wire. Bend the wires in half to form a loop on each side of the original loop. Twist the wires together and tighten the twists with needle-nosed pliers.

6. Extend the wires downward. Slide three assorted green seed, one bugle, and four assorted green seed beads onto each wire. Twist the wires together below the bottom beads.

7. Repeat Steps 2–6 to make two more fern-style leaves (3 leaves are needed).

To Make the Margarita Sprays and Fern-style Leaves Bouquet:

1. Arrange the margarita sprays and fern-style leaves into a bouquet and twist the wires together.

2. Wire the velvet leaves onto the margarita sprays and fern-style leaves and trim the wires with wire cutters.

3. Wrap the twisted wires with florist tape for a finished look.

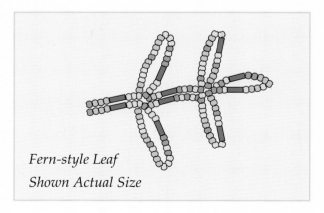

Fern-style Leaf
Shown Actual Size

Change of Heart Hanger

An Assortment of Seed and Specialty Beads:
 Any Size and Color or
 Combination of Sizes and Colors

24-gauge Wire: Silver

Wire Cutters

Needle-nosed Pliers

SENTIMENT

Using the instructions given for the Dream Script on page 70, proceed bending a 90" length of 24-gauge wire into the sentiment given. Randomly slide seed and specialty beads onto the length of wire as desired and twist the wire or wrap it around itself to hold the letters in place. Finish the wire ends and bead a separate length of wire as desired to be used as the hanger.

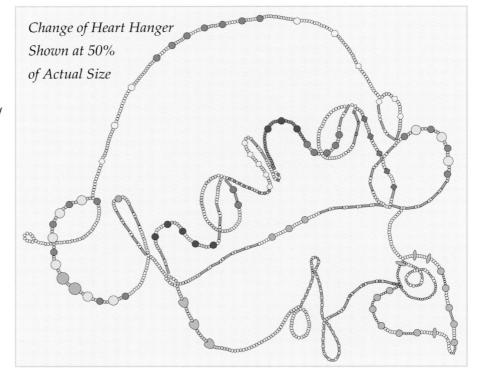

Change of Heart Hanger
Shown at 50%
of Actual Size

DELIGHTFUL ADDITIONS

ew things inspire more than the unexpected detail that takes an object from ordinary to extraordinary. With such special attention given to the little things, that which was once an optional decorating choice now becomes that which is essential.

LONG-STEMMED MUM

Single Mum & Bugle-beaded Berries

Photo on page 102.

Seed Beads, 11/0:
   Silver-lined Gold, 11 containers

Premixed Seed/Bugle Beads: Topaz, 1-oz. jar

Acrylic Paints: Gold, Metallic Bronze

Paintbrush

Silk Leaf Sprays with Berries

14-gauge Wire: Tinned Copper

26-gauge Wire: Silver

Mixing Trays

Tacky Craft Glue & Glue Brush

Découpage Medium & Foam Brush

Wire Cutters

Needle-nosed Pliers

Instructions

To Make the Mum:

1.   Cut the 26-gauge wire with wire cutters into two 30" lengths. Tie a knot at one end of each length of wire.

2.   Slide 20 seed beads onto one of the lengths of wire. Leaving a 6" extension of wire below the first bead, bend the wire so the beads form a loop. Twist the wires together just below the loop.

3.   Bend the wire up and over the bottom center of the loop. Slide 16 seed beads onto the wire. Bend the wire so the beads form a second loop that rests within the first loop. Twist the wires together just below the loop. Tightly twist the wire just below the bottom of the first loop, enabling the wire to extend evenly with the bottom of the loop.

4.   Slide another 20 beads onto the wire. Bend the wire so the beads form another loop, adjacent to the first set of loops. Snugly wrap the long end of the wire around the bottom of the newest loop, then bend the wire up and over the bottom of the first loop. Repeat Step 3.

5.   Continue making six more double loops in the same manner, anchoring the wire to the previous loop each time (8 double loops are needed). Wire the first and last loops together to make one petal.

6.   Repeat Steps 2–5 to make a second petal.

7.   Arrange one petal on top of the other petal and twist the wires together to form a double-layered petal for the center of the flower.

8. Cut the 14-gauge wire into one 18" length to make a long stem. Bend a small loop at one end of the length of wire with needle-nosed pliers. Using the wires from the double-layered petals, wire the long stem onto the flower center through the loop.

9. Repeat Steps 1–7 to make two larger double-layered petals. Use 60" lengths of wire. For the first loop, slide 40 beads onto one of the lengths of wire. For the second loop, slide 36 beads onto the wire. Before wiring the first and last loops together, slide the petal layer underneath the first two layers. Wire the first and last loops together, then wire the petal layer onto the long stem.

10. Repeat Steps 1–7 to make two even larger double-layered petals. Use 70" lengths of wire. For the first loop, slide 50 beads onto one of the lengths of wire. For the second loop, slide 46 beads onto the wire. Before wiring the first and last loops together, slide the petal layer underneath the previous two layers. Wire the first and last loops together, then wire the petal layer onto the long stem.

11. Repeat Steps 1–7 to make the four largest double-layered petals. Use 80" lengths of wire. For the first loop, slide 60 beads onto one of the lengths of wire. For the second loop, slide 56 beads onto the wire. Proceed as in Step 10 to wire the petal layers onto the long stem.

12. Cut the 14-gauge wire into three more 18" lengths. Arrange these wires around the long stem, making certain the loops on the lengths of

wire are at the opposite end, facing downward. Secure the wires together to create a thick, sturdy stem.

13. Cut the 26-gauge wire into one 90" length. Attach the wire to the bottom of the mum at one side of the stem.

14. Slide seed beads onto the wire for a length of 3". Very tightly wrap the beaded wire around the stem, then slide additional seed beads onto the wire for a length of 3". Continue to wrap the beaded wire around the stem, adding more beads as needed to cover the stem. Wrap the wire through the loops at the bottom of the stem several times to secure.

Using the instructions given for the Terra-cotta Mini Vase on pages 14–15, proceed gluing the premixed seed/bugle beads onto the berries on the silk leaf sprays with the tacky craft glue. Lightly paint the berries with one coat of metallic bronze paint and let dry. Seal the berries with one coat of découpage medium. Lightly accent each silk leaf with gold paint and let dry.

DAISY BOUQUET

aisies of Gold

Seed Beads, 11/0:
  Black, Light Gold,
  Spearmint Green,
  1 container each

26-gauge Wire: Silver

Plaid Ribbon, 1½"-wide:
  Orange/Peach/Green, ¾ yard

Embroidery Floss: Olive Green

Wire Cutters

Needle-nosed Pliers

Instructions

To Make Each Daisy:

1. Cut the 26-gauge wire with wire cutters into three 40" lengths. Tie a knot at one end of each length of wire.

2. Slide 30 light gold seed beads onto one of the lengths of wire. Leaving a 6" extension of wire below the first seed bead, bend the wire to form a loop and twist the wires just below the loop. Tighten the twists with needle-nosed pliers.

3. Bend the wire up and over the bottom center of the loop. Slide 16 light gold seed beads onto the wire. Extend the wire to the top of the loop. Wrap the wire around the center of the top of the loop once. Bend the wire to the back of the loop and tightly wrap it just below the bottom of the loop, enabling the wire to extend evenly with the bottom of the loop.

4. Slide another 30 light gold seed beads onto the wire. Bend the wire to form a second loop. Wrap the long end of the wire around the bottom of the loop, then around the bottom of the first loop. Repeat Step 3.

5. Continue forming seven more loops in the same manner, making certain to wrap the wire to the previous loop each time (9 loops are needed). Wire the first and last loops together.

6. Cut the 26-gauge wire into one 10" length. Tie a knot at one end of the length of wire.

7.   Refer to the General Instructions for Forming a Leaf or Flower Petal with a Basic Axis on pages 10–11. Slide four black seed beads onto the length of wire, positioning the bead 2" below the knot. Proceed with forming the center axis.

8.   Form one beaded row of black seed beads and wrap them around the center axis.

9.   Slip the cluster of black seed beads through the center of the nine daisy petals and twist the wires together. Tighten the twists with needle-nosed pliers.

10. Wrap the twisted wires with embroidery floss for a finished look.

11. Repeat Steps 1–10 to make two more daisies (3 daisies are needed).

Daisy
Shown Actual Size

To Make the Fern-style Leaves:

1.   Refer to the instructions for making the Fern-style Leaves on page 100. Use three 36" lengths of wire and slide 30 spearmint green seed beads onto the wire to form the first loop. Separate the wires and slide 14 spearmint green seed beads onto each wire.

2.   Continue forming more loops in the same manner until the leaves are the desired length.

3.   Repeat Steps 1 and 2 to make four more fern-style leaves (5 leaves are needed).

4.   Wrap the twisted wires with embroidery floss for a finished look.

To Make the Daisy and Fern-style Leaves Bouquet:

1.   Arrange the daisies and fern-style leaves into a bouquet and secure the embroidery floss-wrapped stems with a length of wire.

2.   Tie a piece of plaid ribbon into a bow around the bouquet.

SACHET

Apricot Rose Sachet

Seed Beads, 11/0:
   Cream Soda, Forest Green,
   Iced Tea, Melon, Moss Green,
   1 container each

Seed Beads, tiny holeless:
   Clear, 1 bag

26-gauge Wire: Green

26-gauge Wire: Silver

Velvet Leaves, 1" x 1 $\frac{1}{2}$":
   3 Pink/Green, 3 Blue/Green

Silk Ribbon, 7mm:
   Olive Green, $\frac{1}{2}$ yard

Mixing Tray

Tacky Craft Glue
   & Glue Brush

Découpage Medium
   & Foam Brush

Knitting Needle

Wire Cutters

Needle-nosed Pliers

Using the instructions given to make rose petals on pages 80–81, proceed making six rose petals with cream soda, iced tea, and melon seed beads on silver 26-gauge wire. Make two of the petals with six beaded rows and the remaining four petals with five beaded rows. Use a knitting needle to mold the center petal vertically so it wraps around itself and looks like a petal just beginning to open. Make three different sized leaves with forest green and moss green seed beads on green 26-gauge wire. Using the instructions given to make frosted velvet leaves on page 23, glue the clear tiny holeless seed beads onto the three pink/green velvet leaves. Wire the frosted velvet leaves to the rose and leaves. Wrap the twisted wire stems with silk ribbon for a finished look and attach the single rose stem to a sachet.

FLUTTERING FRIEND

$\mathcal{A}$urora Borealis Butterfly Pin

2 Teardrop-shaped Beads, 22mm x 10mm:
  Purple Aurora Borealis

2 Oval Beads, 14mm x 10mm:
  Purple Aurora Borealis

1 Elongated Bead, 40mm x 8mm: Purple

1 Round Bead, 8mm: Purple Aurora Borealis

16-gauge Wire: Silver

20-gauge Wire: Silver

Wire Cutters

Needle-nosed Pliers

Instructions

1.   Cut the 16-gauge wire with wire cutters into one 30" length.

2.   Slide one oval bead onto the length of wire, positioning the bead 6" from one end. Wrap the 6" length of wire around the bead $3\frac{1}{2}$ times with needle-nosed pliers. Secure the end of the wire by bending it around the wire coming from the top of the bead.

3.   Slide the teardrop-shaped bead onto the long wire. Wrap the wire around the bead $3\frac{1}{2}$ times. Leaving a $\frac{1}{8}$" gap, slide the remaining teardrop-shaped bead onto the wire. Wrap the wire around the bead $3\frac{1}{2}$ times.

4.   Slide the remaining oval bead onto the wire. Wrap the wire around the bead $3\frac{1}{2}$ times. Secure the end of the wire by bending it around the wire coming from the top of the bead. Trim away the excess wire.

5.   Cut the 20-gauge wire into one 8" length.

6.   Anchor the wire between the wings and slide the elongated bead onto the wire. Bend the wire up and over the elongated bead in a decorative manner. Wrap the wire between the wings three times.

7.   Slide the round bead onto the wire. Wrap the wire between the wings and bend the wire upward.

8.   Cut the 16-gauge wire into one $6\frac{1}{2}$" length.

9.   Shape the wire into antennae and secure the antennae in place with the wire at the top of the round bead. Trim away the excess wire.

THE BEADED STUDIO

*T*ake a fanciful stroll through our collection of beaded inspirations, created by several exceptional beadwork artists. Necklaces to tiaras, handbags and evening purses, keepsakes for the one you love. Perhaps one of their treasures will arouse your own creative ideas. Enjoy!

Mary Jo Hiney works as a freelance author and designer in the fabric and craft industry, gladly sharing skill-filled secrets gathered over a lifetime of experience. Since the summer of 1991 and under the generous guidance of Jo Packham, owner of Chapelle, Ltd., Mary Jo has been able to explore many new creative categories. Focusing on gifts and decorative accessories, her one-of-a-kind pieces display beauty always enhanced with function.

Mary Jo is the author of *Fabulous Fabrics, Beautiful Foundation-Pieced Quilt Blocks, Creating with Lace, Decorative Fabric-Covered Boxes, Ribbon Basics, Romantic Fabric-Covered Boxes, Romantic Silk Ribbon Keepsakes, Two-Hour Vests,* and *Victorian Ribbon and Lacecrafts Designs.*

MARY JO HINEY

For Evan
To the assurance and
certainty of hope,
the reward of perseverance
in good times and bad.

Mary Jo extends a special thanks to all the talented artists who took the time to send their artwork and photos for the studio gallery in this book. The incredible skill and mastery they show through their art is truly an inspiration.

Diane Fitzgerald is a bead artist who works in a variety of contemporary beading techniques, including what is traditionally considered beadwork using seed beads and bead assemblage with larger beads. Since 1989, she has taught a wide range of bead classes at her shop, Beautiful Beads, in Minneapolis, Minnesota, and around the country. As a bead collector, she specializes in contemporary art glass beads, particularly American, European, and Japanese. She has spent time in the Czech Republic and Germany learning about the glass bead industry and meeting beadmakers from those countries. Diane is the author of *Contemporary Beadwork I: Counted and Charted Patterns for Flat Peyote Stitch* and the coauthor with Helen Banes of *Beads and Threads: A New Technique for Fiber Jewelry.* Through beads, she is able to explore the colors, shapes, and textures that she finds fascinating. Her trademark is simple—she likes to make beautiful things that aren't witty and don't have a message. Her creations are meant to delight and be enjoyed.

DIANE
FITZGERALD

Jackie Hirsh found her creative self four years ago after years as a high school French teacher and psychiatric social worker. Since that time she has been making beadwork and says that it provides her with a loving connection to her late mother and grandmother, both of whom did beautiful handwork. It was actually during the early days of her beading obsession that got her in touch with memories when she was just six or seven years old of her mother beading handbags. She loved parading around with those bejeweled purses which are the inspiration for the handbags and evening purses she creates today.

JACKIE HIRSH

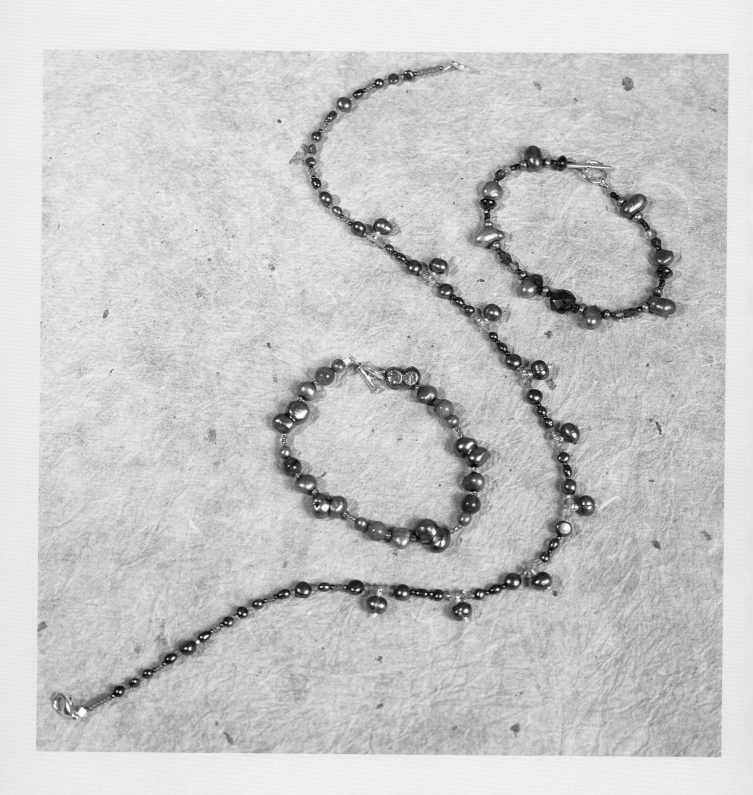

SACRED CHARMS

Sacred Charms designers, Sheyen deLuz and Rosemary Sinclair are inspired by the power of ancient symbols and intricate patterns found in nature. Both are influenced by the feeling of wearing jewelry that is both beautiful and consciously crafted with a message. Their vision encompasses current trends with fresh, forward design and construction using sacred wood, luminous pearls, sterling silver, and the beauty of semiprecious gemstones. Each piece in the Sacred Charms Collection is handcrafted in their design studio in San Diego, California.

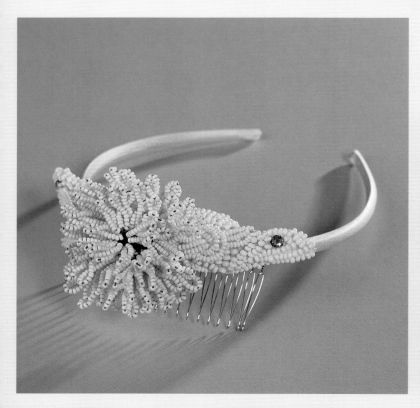

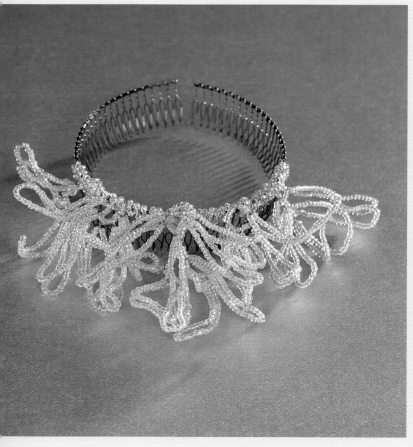

Leah Chalfen worked as a millinery designer for the last four years, but broke ranks this past year and started Leah C. Couture Millinery in order to break away from the industry's traditional millinery forms and offer stylish self-assured women a fashionable way to express themselves. After assisting the head milliner of the Metropolitan Opera of New York City constructing and finishing hats and headpieces for several productions, she is currently designing her own line of hats, bridal headpieces, and hair accessories. All of Leah's designs are originals, made by hand in her West Village Studio.

LEAH CHALFEN

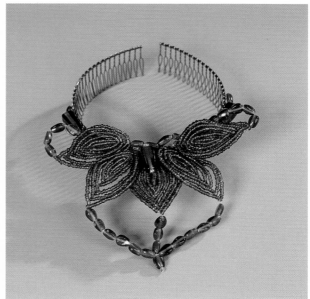

Christiana Lapatina Johnson is a California-based designer with extensive experience in hand beadwork appliqué and print design. She has found her niche offering the impossible at a reasonable price as a life-style manufacturer. The success of Christiana's patchwork jackets and beaded vests led to developing her own company. Following the success of her European premiere in 1997, the fashion community took notice and the doors to the finest specialty and department stores opened worldwide. Internationally the Christiana name has the prestige of being honored with world famous designers such as Christian Dior and Fendi. Unique in her design approach, she has a special style that transforms beautiful glass beads into visual works of art inspired by her extensive travels abroad. All of her frames, lamps, pillows, and albums work together to complement any home. She has always been an enthusiast of Hollywood glamour and couture designers, thus creating the beaded bag, belt, or baguette for any occasion.

CHRISTIANA JOHNSON

GINGER SIZEMORE

Ginger Sizemore is an artist originally from Colorado. She now lives with her husband Sherman and their exotic parrots and macaws on a macadamia nut farm on the Big Island of Hawaii. When she was a child, she was fascinated with two things—her mother's box of buttons and her father's seashell collection. These two elements sparked her interest in jewelry making, and as a child, she would make necklaces and sell them on consignment in local shops. After graduation from high school, Ginger had the opportunity to move to Hawaii where she began her own seashell collection and continued to create jewelry and wearable art. She fulfilled her dream of owning her own store, but after sixteen years has retired from retail. She now enjoys teaching jewelry making and continues to create one-of-a-kind art which she supplies to local boutiques and galleries.

INCHES TO MILLIMETRES AND CENTIMETRES

MM-Millimetres   CM-Centimetres

INCHES	MM	CM	INCHES	CM	INCHES	CM
$1/8$	3	0.9	9	22.9	30	76.2
$1/4$	6	0.6	10	25.4	31	78.7
$3/8$	10	1.0	11	27.9	32	81.3
$1/2$	13	1.3	12	30.5	33	83.8
$5/8$	16	1.6	13	33.0	34	86.4
$3/4$	19	1.9	14	35.6	35	88.9
$7/8$	22	2.2	15	38.1	36	91.4
1	25	2.5	16	40.6	37	94.0
$1^1/4$	32	3.2	17	43.2	38	96.5
$1^1/2$	38	3.8	18	45.7	39	99.1
$1^3/4$	44	4.4	19	48.3	40	101.6
2	51	5.1	20	50.8	41	104.1
$2^1/2$	64	6.4	21	53.3	42	106.7
3	76	7.6	22	55.9	43	109.2
$3^1/2$	89	8.9	23	58.4	44	111.8
4	102	10.2	24	61.0	45	114.3
$4^1/2$	114	11.4	25	63.5	46	116.8
5	127	12.7	26	66.0	47	119.4
6	152	15.2	27	68.6	48	121.9
7	178	17.8	28	71.1	49	124.5
8	203	20.3	29	73.7	50	127.0

YARDS TO METRES

YARDS	METRES	YARDS	METRES	YARDS	METRES	YARDS	METRES	YARDS	METRES
$1/8$	0.11	$2^1/8$	1.94	$4^1/8$	3.77	$6^1/8$	5.60	$8^1/8$	7.43
$1/4$	0.23	$2^1/4$	2.06	$4^1/4$	3.89	$6^1/4$	5.72	$8^1/4$	7.54
$3/8$	0.34	$2^3/8$	2.17	$4^3/8$	4.00	$6^3/8$	5.83	$8^3/8$	7.66
$1/2$	0.46	$2^1/2$	2.29	$4^1/2$	4.11	$6^1/2$	5.94	$8^1/2$	7.77
$5/8$	0.57	$2^5/8$	2.40	$4^5/8$	4.23	$6^5/8$	6.06	$8^5/8$	7.89
$3/4$	0.69	$2^3/4$	2.51	$4^3/4$	4.34	$6^3/4$	6.17	$8^3/4$	8.00
$7/8$	0.80	$2^7/8$	2.63	$4^7/8$	4.46	$6^7/8$	6.29	$8^7/8$	8.12
1	0.91	3	2.74	5	4.57	7	6.40	9	8.23
$1^1/8$	1.03	$3^1/8$	2.86	$5^1/8$	4.69	$7^1/8$	6.52	$9^1/8$	8.34
$1^1/4$	1.14	$3^1/4$	2.97	$5^1/4$	4.80	$7^1/4$	6.63	$9^1/4$	8.46
$1^3/8$	1.26	$3^3/8$	3.09	$5^3/8$	4.91	$7^3/8$	6.74	$9^3/8$	8.57
$1^1/2$	1.37	$3^1/2$	3.20	$5^1/2$	5.03	$7^1/2$	6.86	$9^1/2$	8.69
$1^5/8$	1.49	$3^5/8$	3.31	$5^5/8$	5.14	$7^5/8$	6.97	$9^5/8$	8.80
$1^3/4$	1.60	$3^3/4$	3.43	$5^3/4$	5.26	$7^3/4$	7.09	$9^3/4$	8.92
$1^7/8$	1.71	$3^7/8$	3.54	$5^7/8$	5.37	$7^7/8$	7.20	$9^7/8$	9.03
2	1.83	4	3.66	6	5.49	8	7.32	10	9.14

INDEX

We would like to acknowledge
the following companies:

Art Accents
    960 Yew St., Bellingham, WA 98226
    (877) 733-8989 • www.artaccents.net
Artistic Wire
    752 N. Larch Ave., Elmhurst, IL 60126
    (630) 530-7567 • www.artisticwire.com
Beadbox
    10135 E. Via Linda, Suite C-116,
    Scottsdale, AZ 85258
Beautiful Beads (Diane Fitzgerald)
    115 Hennepin Ave.,
    Minneapolis, MN 55401 • (612) 333-0170
Christiana
    21354 Nordhoff St., Suite 113,
    Chatsworth, CA 91311 • (818) 993-5678
D & CC
    428 S. Zelta, Wichita, KS 67207
    (800) 835-3013
Fairfield
    P.O. Box 1157, Danbury, CT 06813
    (800) 243-0989
Hirsh, Jackie
    1895 Lake Ave., Highland Park, IL 60035
    (847) 432-4648
Leah C. Couture Millinery New York
    118 Washington Place,
    New York, NY 10014 • (212) 807-0699
Mary Jo Hiney Designs
    P.O. Box 6205, Los Osos, CA 93412
    (805) 528-7626
Mill Hill
    P.O. Box 1060, Janesville, WI 53547
    (608) 754-9466 • www.millhill.com
Rings & Things
    P.O. Box 450, Spokane, WA 99210
    (800) 366-2156 • www.Rings-Things.com
Ruban Et Fleur
    8655 S. Sepulveda Blvd.,
    Los Angeles, CA 90045 • (310) 641-3466
Sacred Charms
    364 2nd Street, Suite 7B,
    Encinitas, CA 92024 • (760) 436-2627
Scotticrafts
    550 Franklin Ave., Mt. Vernon, NY 10550
    (800) 862-8721
Susan Clark Originals
    653 Jackson St., Red Bluff, CA 96080
    (530) 527-1383